In memory

Tati

7 Day

NTERREGIONAL
ME AND JUSTICE
ARCH INSTITUTE

UNTRIES

Publication No. 61
Rome, 1998

United Nations Interregional Crime
and Justice Research Institute

Officer-in-Charge: Alberto Bradanini

United Nations Publication
Sales No. E.99.III.N.1

ISBN 9 290 78037-1

Text revision
 Oksanna Hatalak

Publication layout and graphic design
 Roberto Gaudenzi

*This volume was made possible thanks to the generous contribution
of the Ministry of Foreign Affairs of The Netherlands.*

TABLE OF CONTENTS

Page

Preface   i

Chapter 1
Countries in Transition: Why Compare?   1

Chapter 2
Methodology of the International Crime Victim
Survey in Countries in Transition   13

Chapter 3
Victimisation Experience: An Overview   31

Chapter 4
Corruption in Public Administration and Consumer
Fraud   45

Chapter 5
Citizens and Police: Confidence Building in the
Process of Democratisation   63

Chapter 6
Appraisal of Security and Criminal Justice   81

Chapter 7
Summary and Discussion   95
Конспект и Обсуждение   107

**Selected Key Publications on the International Crime
Victim Survey**   121

List of UNICRI Publications and Staff Papers   125

PREFACE

This volume, which I have the privilege to present to the reader, is another in the series of publications reporting the results of the International Crime Victim Survey (ICVS) which to date has been carried out three times (1989, 1992-94, and 1996-97) in almost 60 countries all over the world and which has asked more than 130,000 people about their experience with conventional crime, law enforcement, victim assistance, and crime prevention, as well as about their attitudes towards punishment. It is not an exaggeration to say that the ICVS is the largest international comparative and empirical research currently underway. UNICRI takes pride in having participated in it since 1990 and in being in charge of promoting, carrying out and co-ordinating the ICVS in the developing world and in countries in transition. Our partners in this endeavour - the Ministry of Justice of the Netherlands and the UK Home Office - co-ordinated the ICVS in the industrialised world.

This - as the author calls it - "little book" is the first in a series exclusively devoted to criminal victimisation in countries in transition. It is a synthesis of the results of the ICVS carried out in countries in transition in the second (1992-94) and third (1996-97) sweeps, in which six and then twenty countries in transition respectively took part. This "little book" is accompanied by "a big one" – *International Crime Victim Survey in Countries in Transition: National Reports* - also published by UNICRI and edited by UNICRI staff (Oksanna Hatalak, Anna Alvazzi del Frate and Ugljesa Zvekic) which presents the national reports of all the twenty countries in transition that participated in the third sweep of the ICVS. Therefore, the reader is asked to consult the "big book" for data and their interpretation within a national context; "the little" book, in addition to providing a synthesis and discussing a number of key findings, attempts to contextualise the criminal victimisation experience of citizens from countries in transition within an international comparative perspective. I would also like to draw the reader's attention to UNICRI's bilingual (English-French) *Issues & Reports* series, of which No.11, prepared by U. Zvekic and B. Stankov, presents the results of the ICVS findings for the Balkan region, together with the discussion and recommendations of the Seminar held in Bulgaria in February this year. In addition, attention is drawn both to the previous publications of the ICVS series referred to in Chapter 1 of this volume, as well as to the most recent ones: P. Mayhew and J.J.M. van Dijk (1997) *Criminal Victimisation in Eleven Industrialised Countries* and A. Alvazzi del Frate (1998) *Victims of Crime in the Developing World*. These four most recent books make cross reference to one another and provide a very comprehensive international comparative picture on experiences of victimisation by conventional crime around the world. Interested readers may wish to consult them.

This "little book" discusses several key issues, of which two are of particular importance: corruption in public administration, and the relationship between citizens and the police. Both are, rightly so, discussed within the framework of "confidence building in the process of democratisation". Indeed, in my view, levels of victimisation by conventional crime, risks and costs of crime, and attention to victims of crime - in particular their treatment as well as that of citizens at large by public administration, including law enforcement - all need to be examined in appreciating the efforts and achievements of political and economic reform undertaken by what are nowadays conventionally called countries in transition.

Given the United Nations Crime Prevention and Criminal Justice Programme's most recent emphasis on transnational organised crime, UNICRI, being the research component of the Programme, also places much emphasis on international research on transnational organised crime, including trafficking in human beings, corruption, the world report on organised crime, environmental crimes and alike. While continuing its involvement in the ICVS, UNICRI will also utilise the enormous experience gained with the ICVS to explore transnational organised crime issues. These new research projects, coupled with the ICVS, will provide for a more comprehensive and global understanding of crime and criminal victimisation including their reflections and impact in countries in transition. In this endeavour, the ICVS in general and the ICVS in countries in transition in particular, and thus this "little book" too, are but important building blocks to be cherished, continued, further developed, and integrated into a truly global international perspective.

I wish to express my deepest gratitude to the Ministry of Foreign Affairs and the Ministry of Justice of the Netherlands for their continuous support to the ICVS, and on this occasion in particular, for providing the bulk of the financial support to the ICVS in countries in transition. My gratitude also goes to the UK Home Office for its continuous support, particularly for two participating countries, as well as to the UNDP Country Programme in Kyrgyzstan.

Rome, September 1998   *Alberto Bradanini*
Officer-in-Charge

CHAPTER 1

Countries in Transition: Why Compare?

This little book[1] provides a synthesis of the results of the International Crime Victim Survey (ICVS) carried out in countries in transition. It is accompanied by a much larger volume – *International Crime Victim Survey in Countries in Transition: National Reports* - edited by Hatalak, Alvazzi del Frate and Zvekic (UNICRI, 1998), presenting national reports from twenty countries in transition that took part in the third sweep of the ICVS (1996-97). Summaries of the results regarding six countries in transition which also took part in

---

1   *This little book could not have been written without the dedicated work of the national co-ordinators and their teams in the countries in transition. Their work is fully acknowledged and appreciated in the accompanying "big" book. Special thanks are due to Jan van Dijk of the Dutch Ministry of Justice/University of Leiden, who for years has been a leading force in this joint endeavour - the ICVS -; to Pat Mayhew of the Home Office, UK, and to my colleague at UNICRI, Anna Alvazzi del Frate. Gratitude also goes to Oksanna Hatalak of UNICRI for her patient work in editing the manuscript.*

the second sweep of the ICVS (1992-94) are presented in a previous UNICRI volume – *Understanding Crime: Experiences of Crime and Crime Control* - edited by Alvazzi del Frate, Zvekic and van Dijk (UNICRI, 1993). Thus, these three volumes need to be consulted by those readers interested in details regarding criminal victimisation in countries in transition.

One of the main reasons for publishing this volume is that the results of the 1989, 1992 and 1996 sweeps of the ICVS regarding the industrialised countries were presented in previous publications by van Dijk, Mayhew and Killias (*Experiences of Crime Across the World*, Kluwer, 1990), van Dijk and Mayhew (*Criminal Victimisation in the Industrialised World: Key Findings of the 1989 and 1992 International Crime Survey*, WODC, 1992) and Mayhew and van Dijk (*Criminal Victimisation in Eleven Industrialised Countries*, WODC, 1997). As regards the results of the ICVS in the developing world, two volumes dealt with them: Zvekic and Alvazzi del Frate (*Criminal Victimisation in the Developing World*, UNICRI, 1995) and Alvazzi del Frate (*Victims of Crime in the Developing World*, UNICRI, 1998). Therefore, this is the first time that two volumes are exclusively devoted to the ICVS results in countries in transition, i.e. - as mentioned above - this little one and its accompanying big one.

Countries in transition are somewhat late arrivals to the ICVS since in the first sweep of 1989 only Warsaw (Poland) joined the Survey which was, with the exception of Warsaw and Surabaya (Indonesia) exclusively carried out in the industrialised world. With UNICRI joining the ICVS in 1990, it expanded to include in its second sweep (1992-94) - in addition to the industrialised countries - thirteen developing countries and six countries in transition. Although they were late arrivals, countries in transition made their way in the ICVS to become the largest group participating in the third sweep

(1996-97). The number of industrialised countries and developing countries remained more or less the same in the second and third sweeps of the ICVS while the participation of countries in transition increased more than three times. As a matter of fact, the third sweep of the ICVS covered all but two Central and Eastern European countries[2] as well as Mongolia and Kyrgyzstan.

This by no means happened by mere chance. Although this volume is only about victimisation by conventional crime in countries in transition, and thus does not deal with another major crime issue - organised (transnational) crime - a few considerations of a historical, political and economic nature are in place.

Changes in the political and economic arrangements in the post-communist countries following the fall of the Berlin Wall (1989) attracted the attention of the international community, and in particular donors from the West. From an ideological point of view, the downfall of communism meant that the typical model of the West - in short, pluralistic democracy, a market economy and individual human rights - survived the historical test on the eve of the new millennium. Globalisation and regional integration (particularly in Europe) meant that new political entities and economic markets that emerged from the downfall of the communist system and its national and regional political and economic arrangements require internal changes to facilitate their integration within the new global and

---

2   Bosnia and Herzegovina did not participate since it was felt that the ICVS approach and methodology was not fit to deal with situations which in no way can be characterised as normal due to the tragic conflict in the period 1992-95. Moldova was not included since at the time of preparatory activities for the third sweep it was difficult to identify a local partner that would provide sufficient guarantees that the Survey would be carried out according to the prescribed standards of ICVS. It is hoped that both countries will participate in the next sweep of the ICVS.

3

regional integrative arrangements. Bilateral and multilateral international assistance is seen as a *conditio sine qua non* both by the international community and by the recipient post-communist countries.

International assistance is triggered by a set of interrelated factors. Two appear to be of particular significance. On the one hand, new markets were created after the downfall of communism and new market opportunities appeared. Any return to the previous regime would hamper the exploitation of newly created opportunities as well as political and economic integration both at the regional and global levels. Promoting democracy and the rule of law is also seen as a *conditio sine qua non* for the achievement of new objectives and to prevent a return to the old. This is not to say that the international community and individual donors from the West merely imposed their particular interests. People and new political and economic leadership in countries in transition share, to a large extent, the above-mentioned objectives. Thus, an implicit and often explicit international consensus was reached about a need to deliberately promote changes in the direction of a market economy, pluralistic democracy, rule of law and individual human rights.

The term "countries in transition" is not the happiest one. Often those from what are now conventionally called countries in transition object to this term, sometimes for historical and political reasons such as that the past ideology claimed that their societies are in transition towards communism, and often because it appears that these countries are of a "second order". Others, such as developing countries, claim that they are also countries in transition - and rightly so. Even a number of industrialised countries claim that they are in transition from certain long-lasting political arrangements (monopolistic position of certain political parties or groups within a pluralistic political set up; from centralisation towards decentralisation, etc.) and from a large share of state ownership in national economy towards privatisation. In this sense, a search for political alternatives and privatisation is not the exclusive trademark of what are conventionally called countries in transition. Yet, there are at least three important considerations which may facilitate the classification of heterogeneous countries under the label of countries in transition.

First, their common political and economic heritage which, for some of them, goes far beyond the socialist period of their history. Many of these countries share the Slavic origin of their peoples; some of these, before the end of the First World War, belonged to the three great empires of the time: the Austro-Hungarian, the Ottoman and the Russian Empires; in most of them the majority of the peoples are Catholic or Orthodox Christians. Moreover, the states of some of them were created after the First World War, such as the former Czechoslovakia or the former Yugoslavia. Yet, the most influential factor in their more recent history was their belonging to the communist world, which lasted for some three quarters of a century for some and for almost half a century for others; this is by no means a short period of time. All these countries shared a common political ideology of socialism/communism; their political set-up was that of political decision-making resting within one party – a communist one - with a variety of names and organisational arrangements. Their economic system was based on state/social property - again with a number of variations and varying degrees of autonomy of economic actors, including the magnitude of the private sector economy. Many of them belonged to regional military-political (the Warsaw Pact) and economic-trade regional and bilateral arrangements. Out of twenty countries participating in the third sweep of the ICVS, eight were part of the former USSR (some are now in a loose grouping of the Commonwealth of Independent States); five were federal entities of the former Yugoslavia, and two composed the former Czechoslovakia. All of them gained their independence in the early '90s; some peacefully but not without tensions (the former USSR Republics; the Czech and Slovak Republics; and the Former Yugoslav Republic of Macedonia) and the rest of the Republics of the former Socialist Federal Republic of Yugoslavia through violent conflict. Thus, those eight countries that emerged following the downfall of their previous federal/confederal set-ups have an even stronger core common heritage than others labelled countries in transition. The only example of complete integration following the fall of the Berlin Wall is, at present, that of the former Democratic Republic of Germany into the Federal Republic of Germany.

The common political and economic heritage that, to a certain degree, groups them together also determines to a large extent their similar future – unwillingly perhaps but decisively so. Indeed, it is well established that the process of change which all of these countries are undergoing shares, to varying degrees, a number of similarities in terms of objectives, methods and problems. This is not the place to discuss them at any length. Nevertheless, victimisation by conventional crime (which the ICVS deals with) and threats by organised (transnational) crime (which the ICVS does not deal with although it provides some useful indications on the issue) deserve special attention. Moreover, it is important to underline that in terms of legal reform most of the countries in transition are members both of the United Nations and of the Council of Europe. To a large extent, this membership influences the directions of legal reform, particularly in terms of the reception of international standards in national constitutional, administrative, labour, family, commercial and criminal law as well as adherence to international and regional conventions. Paradoxically, similarities of the past legal systems will be replaced by similarities in the new legal system resulting from the sharing of the same political, economic and legal paradigm, as well as membership in international and regional organisations. Moreover, aspirations to become members of the European Union will further enhance similarities within what are now labelled countries in transition and with, at least, the present fifteen members of the European Union. NATO's Partnership for Peace is yet another important link in the newly emerged chain of integrative processes "replacing" the old ones.

What distinguishes countries in transition as a group is that change is deliberate. Deliberate social change is a particular characteristic of modernisation, but it appears that the degree of the purpose of change was nowhere as high as in countries in transition, at least in the more recent times. This paradoxically applies both to their transition into a socialist system as well as to their efforts to pull away from the socialist system. In both cases, international assistance played an important role, although in the former it was limited to the "first country of communism" and the rest of "brotherly countries and parties" while nowadays, in the latter, it is wider both in terms of types of actors as well as their geographical spread. Thus, the above-mentioned international assistance to countries in transition is an integral part of the deliberate transition as is membership in international and regional organisations and arrangements. The participation of countries in transition in international programmes and projects is also a part of this deliberate change. The ICVS is not an exception.

These considerations are not meant to downplay differences among those countries that appear to be particularly marked nowadays and regard both the starting position on their path towards modern market-oriented and democratic states, as well as the depth and magnitude of change achieved in the last decade. Thus, in terms of the level of economic development, there are clear differences between, for instance, Poland and Albania as there are differences in terms of their political history before and during the communist regime (e.g. the level of democracy in Czechoslovakia during the period of the two Great Wars and that of some other countries; the rebellions against the communist regime such as those in Poland and Hungary; the closeness of their political and economic links with the former Soviet Union such as the quite independent former Yugoslavia and Albania and others which were fully fledged members of the Eastern European military-political and economic block, etc). Finally, nowadays there are quite marked differences within this group of countries in terms of achieved level of market economy, privatisation, GNP per capita and political democracy.

Above and beyond the above-mentioned considerations, the participation of countries in transition in the ICVS was prompted by the main aims of the ICVS in general. While these are dealt with in greater detail in the next chapter, it will suffice here to mention several peculiarities regarding countries in transition. Despite the inadequacy of criminal justice statistics for comparing crime in different countries, in many ex-communist countries these were not available to either the national public or to the international community for long periods of time. Those that were available shared many deficiencies regarding administrative statistics in any country. It is well established that the criminal justice "crime story" differs from the "true crime story". Furthermore, many countries in transition had no experience of victimisation surveys, and the ICVS provided an opportunity to assist in the acquisition of appropriate methodology for research and policy analysis as well as to provide for as large as possible comparison on an international comparative level. It is particularly important to bear in mind that even in totalitarian societies many victims were, and still are, individual households and citizens that bear the risks and costs of crime. Since the ICVS was carried out in countries in transition during the period of transition, much can be learned about those risks and costs. Additionally, the above-mentioned emerging similarities with the industrialised countries also refer to crime concerns. It is by now well established and strongly supported by the evidence provided by the ICVS that crime patterns as well as crime levels in countries in transition are becoming more and more like those of the industrialised world. This, together with the fact that changes in criminal legislation have become more concerned than in the past with crime victims, fully supports efforts to promote victimisation surveys for research, management, policy analysis and partnership in crime prevention. Like many other things in countries in transition, even crime is no longer the sole concern of the state, nor can an effective crime prevention policy rest solely on state agencies and programmes. For citizens to participate in crime prevention, it is indispensable to provide them with reliable and timely information as well as to give them opportunities to have their say both about their own crime concerns as well as about the workings of the criminal justice system. The method of the victimisation survey itself provides such an opportunity which could be expanded to other opportunities such as organised public debates about crime, crime prevention and control. Indeed, following the carrying out of the ICVS in several countries in transition, policy round tables were organised with the participation of the research community, state agencies involved in crime control and prevention (ministries of justice, interior, education, social welfare, health, etc.) and non-governmental organisations.

The ICVS aims to contribute to public debate and transparency about crime and the workings of the criminal justice system, in particular that of law enforcement. Modern and democratic law enforcement needs to be accountable to the public and willing to lend itself to critical appreciation. Thus, there are two particularly important issues in countries in transition, namely, corruption in public administration, and the relationship between citizens and the police. Both stand as political tests of the achievements in the process of reform as related to the rule of law in general, and criminal justice in particular. The process of informed appreciation of the workings of the criminal justice system as a part of public administration in many countries in transition started with the ICVS. Therein lies the ICVS's contribution to democratic reform and rational partnership-based crime prevention. It is hoped that this process will continue, particularly in view of the fact that, as explained in the next chapter on methodology, in most of the countries in transition the ICVS was carried out only in the largest cities, usually the capital. Therefore, there is a need to carry out national as well as local victim surveys. On the basis of the experience gained with the ICVS, it is hoped that policy makers and criminal justice administrators, jointly with the research community and the public at large, will further develop victim surveys, policy analysis and public debate. The participation of what are now termed as countries in transition in future sweeps of the ICVS will be a sign of their further integration in the modern international community and modern trends in crime prevention and its control.

When the factors that now group countries in transition loose their importance, there will be no need for more little or big volumes on criminal victimisation in countries in transition. This is as much to be hoped for as is a reduction in the crime levels and crime risks for citizens of what then perhaps will be referred to as the *former countries in transition*.

CHAPTER 2

Methodology of the International Crime Victim Survey in Countries in Transition

The potential of victim surveys for comparative purposes led to the carrying out of the first International Crime Victim Survey (ICS at the time, later renamed ICVS), in 1989. A first proposal to organise an international victimisation survey was launched by the OECD in the 1970s. Pilot studies were carried out in the USA, the Netherlands and Finland. Further to a meeting of the Standing Conference of Local and Regional Authorities of the Council of Europe, held in 1987 in Barcelona, a working group was created and started developing the survey methodology and questionnaire.[1] Some twenty countries were invited to participate in a standardised victimisation survey.

---

1   The working group which co-ordinated the first International Survey was composed by J.J.M. van Dijk, P. Mayhew and M. Killias.

There were three main reasons for setting up the ICVS. The first was related to the enormous problems with offences recorded by the police for comparing crime in different countries. The second was the lack of any alternative standardised measure, and the third was the promotion of the victim survey in countries that have no, or only a meagre experience of it. All the above-mentioned reasons are fully applicable to countries in transition.

Police figures are inadequate for comparative purposes because the majority of incidents the police become aware of are brought to their attention by victims, and any differences in propensity to report in different countries will influence the comparability of the amount of crime known by the police. Police figures vary because of differences in legal definitions, recording practices, and precise rules for classifying and counting incidents. These limitations are well known.

A number of industrialised countries have launched crime or "victimisation" surveys to gain a wider and better knowledge of national crime problems – and, to a great extent, the ICVS reflects their approach and experience. Such surveys ask representative population samples about selected offences they have experienced over a given time. They deal with incidents that have, or have not, been reported to the police and in particular with the reasons why people do or do not choose to report them to the police. They provide a more realistic record of the population affected by crime and - if the surveys are repeated - a measure of trends in crime unaffected by changes in the victims' reporting behaviour, or by administrative changes in recording crime. Social and demographic information on the respondents also provide an opportunity to analyse types of crime risks and the way they vary for different groups according to a number of factors, such as social status, age, gender, etc.

The experience gained with national and local surveys called for a comparative international survey in view of the fact that the number of countries with appropriate surveys were limited, and the surveys used different methods, thus making comparison far from straightforward.[2]

The ICVS to date

There have been three rounds of the ICVS. The first was developed by a Working Group set up in 1987, leading to fieldwork early in 1989. Thereafter the Working Group reformed, consisting of Jan van Dijk (Ministry of Justice/University of Leiden, the Netherlands; overall co-ordinator), Pat Mayhew (Home Office, United Kingdom), and Ugljesa Zvekic and Anna Alvazzi del Frate of the United Nations Interregional Criminal Justice Research Institute (UNICRI) in Rome.

The second ICVS took place in 1992/94, and the third in 1996/97. In the industrialised countries, each country met its own survey costs, although much of the administrative overheads of the ICVS programme were borne by the Dutch Ministry of Justice, which has also sponsored survey activities in almost all the developing countries and countries in transition. Further financial assistance was provided by the Dutch Ministry of Foreign Affairs, the Home Office, UK, the Department of Justice Canada, the European Institute for Crime Prevention and Control (HEUNI) and UNDP. The Working

---

2   Differences in survey design and administration influence both the amount and type of victimisation measured. The technical differences at issue include: the number of people interviewed in the household; sampling frame and age range; mode of interviewer, "screening" methods and number of "screeners"; "recall" period; and response rates.

15

Groups managed oversight of the surveys, although a co-ordinator in each country was responsible for the conduct of fieldwork and, where necessary, for ensuring a sound translation of the questionnaire. The technical management of most of the surveys in the industrialised countries was carried out by InterView, a Dutch survey company. InterView sub-contracted fieldwork to survey companies in the participating countries, while maintaining responsibility for the questionnaire, sample selection and interview procedures. UNICRI was responsible for the face-to-face questionnaire and for monitoring of the ICVS in the developing countries and countries in transition. The data from the surveys were integrated and processed by John van Kesteren of the Criminological Institute, Faculty of Law of the University of Leiden in the Netherlands.

Fifteen countries took part in the first (1989) ICVS, including the cities of Warsaw (Poland) and Surabaya (Indonesia). The second (1992/94) ICVS covered eleven industrialised countries, thirteen developing countries and six countries in transition. Eight of the countries had taken part in 1989. Full details of the 1989 and 1992 surveys in industrialised countries are reported in van Dijk et al., (1990) and in van Dijk and Mayhew (1992). Further information and reports on the 1992 ICVS, including six countries in transition, are presented in Alvazzi del Frate et al. (1993).

The second (1992/94) round of the ICVS expanded to include standardised surveys in thirteen developing countries and six countries in transition, mainly at the city level. These were taken forward largely by UNICRI which was keen to sensitise governments of developing countries and countries in transition on the dimensions and extent of crime in their urban areas - especially as police data on crime were often poor. Results from the developing world are reported in Zvekic and Alvazzi del Frate (1995). After the second ICVS, a programme of standardised surveys of crime against businesses was also mounted in nine countries. Comparative results are presented in van Dijk and Terlouw (1996).

The third round of the ICVS was carried out in 1996 and 1997 and encompassed eleven industrialised countries, thirteen developing countries and twenty countries in transition. This and the accompanying volume (Hatalak, Alvazzi del Frate and Zvekic, 1998) report the findings related to countries in transition, while the results of the 1996 ICVS for industrialised countries are reported in Mayhew and van Dijk (1997) and, for developing countries, in Alvazzi del Frate (1998).

All in all, with the 1996/97 ICVS, more than 130,000 people were interviewed in 40 languages around the world.

Table 1. International Crime Victim Survey - Overview of participation in the 1989, 1992-94 and 1996-97 "sweeps"

Industrialised countries	1989	1992-94	1996-97
1 Australia	*	*	
2 Austria			*
3 Belgium	*	*	
4 Canada	*	*	*
5 England & Wales	*	*	*
6 Finland	*	*	*
7 France	*		
8 Germany	*		
9 Italy		*	
10 Japan	*		
11 Malta			*
12 The Netherlands	*	*	*
13 New Zealand		*	
14 Northern Ireland	*		*
15 Norway	*		
16 Scotland	*		*
17 Spain	*	*	
18 Sweden		*	*
19 Switzerland	*		*
20 USA	*	*	*

Table 1 (contd.)

Countries in transition	1989	1992-94	1996-97
1 Albania			*
2 Belarus			*
3 Bulgaria			*
4 Croatia			*
5 Czech Republic		*	*
6 Estonia		*	*
7 F. R. of Yugoslavia			*
8 FYR of Macedonia			*
9 Georgia		*	*
10 Hungary			*
11 Kyrgyzstan			*
12 Latvia			*
13 Lithuania			*
14 Mongolia			*
15 Poland	*	*	*
16 Romania			*
17 Russia		*	*
18 Slovak Republic		*	*
19 Slovenia		*	*
20 Ukraine			*

Developing countries	1989	1992-94	1996-97
1 Argentina		*	*
2 Bolivia			*
3 Botswana			*
4 Brazil		*	*
5 China		*	
6 Colombia			*
7 Costa Rica		*	*
8 Egypt		*	
9 India		*	*
10 Indonesia	*	*	*
11 Papua New Guinea		* (°)	
12 Paraguay			*
13 The Philippines		*	*
14 South Africa		*	*
15 Tanzania		*	
16 Tunisia		*	
17 Uganda		*	*
18 Zimbabwe			*

(°) Data set not available

Countries in transition

As regards countries in transition, six countries participated in the 1992-94 ICVS, while twenty countries took part in the 1996-97 sweep. Only Poland (Warsaw) participated in the first sweep (1989)

18

and from then on in both the second and third sweeps of the ICVS. Six countries in transition participated both in the second and third sweeps. It should be noted that, using the conventional classification of industrialised countries, developing countries and countries in transition, the latter group is the largest in terms of number of participating countries. It is also the group that increased threefold from the second to the third sweep of the ICVS.

This is very much the result of the interest of the international community and donors in the reform process towards a market economy and a democratic political system. Moreover, in many communist countries crime statistics were either not available to the public or indeed to the international community, or were considered inadequate. Nor was there much experience with victimisation surveys and in particular citizens' experience with law enforcement and crime prevention. These and other reasons prompted an emphasis on countries in transition, a term which groups together ex-communist countries. Furthermore, the fall of the communist system was accompanied by the dismemberment of the USSR, Czechoslovakia and Yugoslavia, and consequently by the creation of a number of newly independent states.

Table 2. Overview of participation, methodology and languages used in the International Crime Victim Survey in countries in transition

Second ICVS (1992-94)	Date	Sample Size	Urban	Rural	Method	Language
Czechoslovakia: Czech*	1992	1,262	237	1,025	F/F	Czech/Slovak
Czechoslovakia: Slovak*	1992	508	21	487	F/F	Czech/Slovak
Estonia	1993	1,000	457	543	F/F	Estonian
Georgia	1992	1,395			F/F	Russian
Poland	1992	2,033	666	1,367	F/F	Polish
Russia (Moscow)	1992	1,002	1,002		F/F	Russian
Slovenia (Ljubljana)	1992	1,000	1,000		CATI + CAPI**	Slovenian

*   Sample from the survey carried out in the former Czechoslovakia was broken down into Czech and Slovak.

** Computer Assisted Personal Interview.

Table 2 (contd.)

Third ICVS (1996-97)	Date	Sample Size	Urban	Rural	Method	Language
Albania (Tirana)	1996	1,200	983	217	F/F	Albanian
Belarus (Minsk)	1997	999	999		F/F	Belorussian, Russian
Bulgaria (Sofia)	1997	1,076	1,076		F/F	Bulgarian
Croatia (Zagreb)	1997	994	994		F/F	Croatian
Czech Republic	1996	1,801	717	1,084	F/F	Czech
Estonia	1995	1,173	364	809	F/F	Estonian, Russian
Georgia	1996	1,137	567	570	F/F	Russian
Hungary (Budapest)	1996	756	756		F/F	Hungarian
Kyrgyzstan	1996	1,750	1,494	256	F/F	Kyrgyz, Russian, Uzbeck
Latvia	1996	1,411	1,011	400	F/F	Latvian, Russian
Lithuania	1997	1,176	656	520	F/F	Lithuanian, Russian
FYR Macedonia (Skopje)	1996	700	700		F/F	Macedonian
Mongolia (Ulan Baatar)	1996	1,200	1,053	147	F/F	Mongolian
Poland	1996	3,483	2,410	1,073	F/F	Polish
Romania (Bucharest)	1996	1,091	1,000	91	F/F	Romanian
Russia (Moscow)	1996	1,018	1,018		F/F	Russian
Slovak Republic (Bratislava)	1997	1,105	1,105		F/F	Slovak
Slovenia (Ljubljana)	1997	2,053	1,107	946	CATI	Slovenian
Ukraine (Kiev)	1997	1,000	1,000		F/F	Ukrainian, Russian
Yugoslavia (Belgrade)	1996	1,094	1,094		F/F	Serbian

Survey methods

The ICVS was carried out by using two main survey methods: computer assisted telephone interviewing (CATI) and face-to-face. As a rule, CATI was adopted in the industrialised countries, with the exception of Northern Ireland (1989 and 1996), Spain (1993) and Malta (1997), and face-to-face was used in the developing countries and countries in transition, with the only exception of Slovenia (1992 and 1997).

The count of crime

The ICVS enquires about crimes against clearly identifiable individuals, excluding children. While the ICVS looks into incidents which by and large accord with legal definitions of offences, in essence it accepts the accounts that the respondents are prepared to give to the interviewers of what happened. Therefore, the ICVS accepts a broader definition of crime than the police which, once incidents are reported to them, are likely to select those which merit the attention of the criminal justice system, or meet organisational demands and parameters to allow for further processing.

Eleven main forms of victimisation are covered by the ICVS, three of which allow for further grouping. Household crimes are those which can be seen as affecting the household at large, and respondents report on all incidents known to them. For personal crimes, they report on what happened to them personally.

Household property crimes	Personal crime
* theft of car	* theft of personal property
* theft from cars	- pickpocketing
* vandalism to cars	- non-contact personal thefts
* theft of motorcycles	* sexual incidents
* theft of bicycles	- sexual assaults
* burglary with entry	- offensive behaviour
* attempted burglary	* assaults/threats
* robbery	- assaults with force
	- assaults without force

In the surveys in developing countries and countries in transition, consumer fraud and corruption were also covered. Consumer fraud was asked about in the industrialised countries in 1992 and 1996, and corruption in 1996/97.

The respondents are asked first about their experience of crime over the last five years. Those who mention an incident of any particular type are asked when it occurred, and if in the last year, how many times. All victims reporting incidents over the past five years are asked some additional questions about what happened.

Sampling

In countries in transition, samples of 1,000 respondents were generally drawn from the population of the largest city (see Table 2), although in a few countries the survey covered either several cities with or without the addition of a small rural sample (e.g. Estonia) and in Poland in 1996 the national sample was used. Sampling generally started with the identification of administrative zones in the cities, followed by a step-by-step procedure aimed at identifying: 1) areas; 2) streets; 3) blocks; 4) households; and 5) the respondent (a person aged 16 or more whose birthday came next).

Fieldwork included the undertaking of feasibility/training missions and the carrying out of pilot studies in the countries which were participating in the ICVS for the first time, as well as the carrying out of the fully fledged surveys in all participating countries.

Feasibility/training missions

One of the objectives of the missions was to get acquainted with the target country's criminological situation and law enforcement and criminal justice needs in the area of crime prevention. This lead to the identification of specific needs as regards, for example, additional questions to be included in the questionnaire and the development of the sampling design. However, due to the comparative character of the project, the proposed changes were kept within the main structure and content of the standard questionnaire and sampling.

The missions identified and contacted the appropriate structures (university, research institute, public opinion poll company) to be in charge of the fieldwork and established contacts with the *national co-ordinator*, who was appointed in each country to monitor the activities of the local team.

Another aim of the missions was to pass on experience and provide advice as to the technical and organisational aspect of the ICVS, with the assistance of the "Manual" developed by UNICRI for this purpose (Alvazzi del Frate, 1996). Details regarding sampling, translation of the questionnaire into local language(s), organisation of the project, selection and training of the interviewers, data collection method, data entry procedure, data analysis and the structure of the national report were discussed and mutually agreed upon. Training on the conduct of the face-to-face survey and on the use of the ICVS data entry software developed by the University of Leiden was provided to selected members of the local team who, in turn, provided further training to the interviewers.

Furthermore, meetings were held at the Ministry of the Interior or Ministry of Justice of the participating countries, with the police and other authorities, to describe the project, its requirements and potentials in terms of developing crime prevention strategies.

Translation of questionnaire

In some countries the interviewers, having to work in several local dialects, were provided with the translation in the language of the majority linguistic group while translations into dialects were provided on the spot, that is to say, during the interviewing process. It is difficult to assess to what extent this affected the responses, but it does indicate the need for closer monitoring and control of the translation procedure and reliability. Back and forth translation from the original English into and from the language in question was carried out in a number of countries, both to ensure the adequacy of translation as well as to provide for the most appropriate native wording.

Carrying out of the full-fledged survey

In principle, pilots were carried out only in countries that were newcomers to the ICVS. In most of the countries in transition the full-fledged survey was administered during the period January-March 1992 and 1996. However, in some countries the survey was carried out somewhat later in the year.

Data collection lasted from eight to ten weeks in each country and was followed by the data entry and logical validation process. On average, fieldwork lasted four months including translation of the questionnaire, sampling, data collection and preparation of the dataset for delivery. A final report was prepared by each national co-ordinator.

The results in this book are based on data which have been weighted to make the samples as representative as possible of national populations aged 16 or more in terms of gender, regional population distribution, age, and household composition.

Face-to-face interviewing

In most countries the survey was carried out by an *ad hoc* team of interviewers. On average, face-to-face interviews lasted thirty minutes and could generally be understood by illiterate respondents.

Response rates

Face-to-face surveys

A systematic collection of data on response rates and refusals was only initiated with the 1997 version of the face-to-face questionnaire. As regards the previous surveys, information on the response rate was provided by the national co-ordinators in their final reports.

As regards countries in transition, on average the response rate was 81.3%,[3] while the refusal rate was 10.1%. The highest rates of

---

3   *The lowest response rates were observed in Lithuania (53.9%) and the Slovak Republic (55.9%). In all the other countries in transition the response rates were above 73% (Croatia).*

refusal were observed in the Slovak Republic (23.9%), Lithuania (21.3%), Hungary (19.3%), the Czech Republic (17.5%) and Bulgaria (15.3%). It was observed that in some countries in transition the refusal rate was higher due to the vicinity of recent war conflicts, which may have increased the general level of suspicion. In some countries, fear of strangers was so widespread that the national co-ordinator suggested including a series of questions dealing with attitudes towards opening the door to strangers and the use of entryphones.

In some countries (e.g. Croatia, F.R. of Yugoslavia), announcement letters were sent to selected households. Although the majority of those who received such letters in time accepted to be interviewed, some refused to participate in the survey, especially among those living in "high-crime" areas.[4]

Some refused to be interviewed because of mistrust of interviewers and fear for their own security, including a few that declared that they had been crime victims and demonstrated their anger towards the indifference of the police and courts.

It should finally be noted that many co-ordinators pointed out the high level of non-relevant contacts which resulted either in abandoned households (people who had emigrated or left for an

---

4   *In some cases it occurred that some of those who had received announcement letters informed the interviewers that they did not want to participate in the survey. In other cases, the interviewers were denied access to apartments, which frequently occurred in the city areas where multiple-storey buildings with interphones represent the main type of habitation. Finally, a certain number of citizens let the interviewers in, but refused to be interviewed. Those respondents usually invoked "old age" or "illness" as reasons for refusal, which was only sometimes true. Many respondents expressed hostility towards the survey, and stressed that they were interested only in the things that could ameliorate their especially bad material conditions.*

indefinite time), or households that had been transformed into commercial businesses or had even been illegally reconstructed and no longer matched the given address.

Structure of the presentation

This little book follows, to the extent possible, the structure adopted by Mayhew and van Dijk in their volume on *Criminal Victimisation in Eleven Industrialised Countries* (1997). This choice was made in order to ease comparative reading of the results of the ICVS for industrialised countries and countries in transition. A similar structure is adopted by Alvazzi del Frate in her volume on *Victims of Crime in the Developing World* (1998).

Many interesting topics are not included in this volume. The reader is once again directed to consult the accompanying big volume (edited by Hatalak, Alvazzi del Frate and Zvekic, 1998) presenting the national reports of all participating countries in transition.

As noted earlier, this is the first volume in the ICVS series to deal exclusively with countries in transition. The International Working Group adopted a decision to present one-year rates, when appropriate. This resulted in averaging data from the 1992-94 and 1996-97 ICVS for countries that participated in both sweeps. If not specifically mentioned, data pertain to the 1996-97 sweep only, but for the sake of convenience are referred to as the 1996 ICVS. The "big" volume presents the results of the 1996-97 ICVS.

In order to place the results relating to countries in transition in an international context, it was decided to present, whenever appropriate, first an overview of the topic dealt with from the world regions comparative perspective, and then to focus on countries in transition. The International Working Group adopted two classifications:

26

Industrialised countries		Western Europe
Countries in transition	and	New World (USA, Canada, Australia, New Zealand)
Developing countries		Countries in transition
		Africa
		Asia
		Latin America

Both classifications are used for analytical purposes although the second one is used more often than the first. This, in turn, determined the decision to present the results of the ICVS in independent volumes, each dealing with distinct aggregates of countries from the developmental point of view, i.e. industrialised countries, countries in transition, and developing countries.

This volume presents only city or urban area data from the countries in transition. As noted earlier, although in the majority of the countries in transition the ICVS was carried out in the largest - mainly capital - city, there were few exceptions. In addition, given the above-mentioned decision to average one year rates for countries which participated in both sweeps, and in view of the 1992-94 ICVS in countries in transition being carried out in cities only, it was decided for comparative purposes to use city/urban area data only. Consequently, both the title of this little volume as well as references to countries in tables and throughout the text are somewhat misleading since, for example, Russia is Moscow while Poland is Warsaw and other urban areas covered by the Polish ICVS. Yet, for the sake of convenience and to facilitate cross-references to industrialised and developing countries, a decision was made to refer to the country rather than to the city.

Following Chapter 1, which provides some political and historical considerations regarding countries in transition, and this chapter which outlines the history and methodology of the ICVS with a particular focus on countries in transition, Chapter 3 presents rates of victimisation for four main categories of crime. Country crime profiles and trends over time (for six repeat countries only) are also examined.

Chapter 4 is exclusively devoted to corruption in public administration and consumer fraud, the two most diffused forms of victimisation in countries in transition that have to do much more with the relationship between citizens and the state and the consumer and the service economy than with what is usually meant by conventional crime. Yet, the two topics dealt with in Chapter 4 are most indicative of the depth and direction of change in countries in transition as perceived by ordinary citizens.

Chapter 5 presents the results regarding reporting of crime to police, reasons for reporting and non-reporting, and several measures of citizens' satisfaction with police work. However, the chapter does much more than that. Its title "Citizens and Police: Confidence Building in the Process of Democratisation" clearly sets the tone of the enquiry highlighting the significance of trust in law enforcement and satisfaction with the workings of the law enforcement as a first contact point of the criminal justice system. Similarly to the way corruption and consumer fraud were dealt with in the previous chapter, the issues discussed in this chapter often stand as tests for changes achieved and the way they are perceived by citizens and victims of crime.

In Chapter 6, entitled "Appraisal of Security and Criminal Justice", the discussion focuses on fear of crime, crime prevention measures, victim assistance and citizens' most preferred sentence for a 21-year-old recidivist burglar (the punishment orientation).

Finally, Chapter 7 provides a summary and a short discussion on corruption in public administration and the relationship between citizens and the police, two issues considered of great significance in countries in transition when it comes to citizens' appreciation of the system in transition.

References

Alvazzi del Frate, A., Zvekic, U. and van Dijk, J.J.M. (Eds.) (1993). *Understanding Crime: Experiences of Crime and Crime Control.* Rome: UNICRI.

Alvazzi del Frate, A. (1996). *Manual, Face-to-face International Crime (Victim) Survey.* UNICRI.

Alvazzi del Frate, A. (1998). *Victims of Crime in the Developing World.* Rome: UNICRI.

Hatalak, O., Alvazzi del Frate, A. and Zvekic, U. (Eds.) (1998). *International Crime Victim Survey in Countries in Transition: National Reports.* Rome: UNICRI.

Mayhew, P. and van Dijk, J.J.M. (1997). *Criminal Victimisation in Eleven Industrialised Countries.* The Hague: WODC.

Van Dijk, J.J.M., Mayhew, P. and Killias, M. (1990). *Experiences of Crime Across the World: Key Findings from the 1989 International Crime Survey.* Deventer: Kluwer Law and Taxation.

Van Dijk, J.J.M. and Mayhew, P. (1992). *Criminal Victimisation in the Industrialised World: Key Findings of the 1989 and 1992 International Crime Surveys.* The Hague: Ministry of Justice of the Netherlands.

Van Dijk, J.J.M. and Terlouw, G.J. (1996). 'An international perspective of the business community as victims of fraud and crime'. *Security Journal,* October: 157-167.

Zvekic, U. and Alvazzi del Frate, A. (1995). *Criminal Victimisation in the Developing World.* Rome: UNICRI.

CHAPTER 3

Victimisation Experience: An Overview

As noted in the previous chapter, the ICVS covered eleven types of conventional crimes in addition to corruption in public administration and consumer fraud (the latter is dealt with in the following chapter). Victimisation experience is expressed through prevalence rates (the percentage of those aged 16 or over who experienced a specific form of crime once or more) and incidence rates (the number of crimes experienced by each 100 in the sample, taking into account all incidents against victims). For comparative purposes, prevalence rates only are used in this chapter since they reflect fairly well the spread of crime across the urban population. The ICVS provides both for last year estimates (the calendar year preceding the survey) as well as for the last five years.[1] Only findings pertaining to

---

1   *In the initial screening part of the questionnaire the respondents are asked about their victimisation experience over the last five years. Follow-up questions deal with the timing of the incidents, that is, whether it happened in the current year, in the last year or longer ago.*

the last year experience are presented here since there is greater memory loss particularly for less serious incidents that happened longer ago (victimisation rates over five years are much less than five times higher than the calendar year rates).

The results are presented in four crime groups:

- burglary: incidents involving entry into homes by offenders, and attempted burglaries;
- car-related theft: theft of and from cars;
- contact crime: robbery, assault with force and sexual assaults; and
- other crime: bicycle and motorcycle thefts, vandalism to cars, theft of personal property, offensive sexual behaviour and threats.

For comparative purposes, a regional overview will first be provided, followed by a country level presentation within the group of countries in transition.

Burglary

As regards burglary, the highest risk of victimisation exists in Africa and Latin America. Households in the New World are at a somewhat higher risk of being visited by an offender than are those in countries in transition and Western Europe, while the lowest risk exposure is registered in Asia. Patterns regarding attempted burglary closely follow those of completed burglary. However, it should be noted that there were less incidents of attempted burglary in comparison with completed burglary in Asia, while the two are almost equal in countries in transition.

Table 1. Burglary and attempted burglary by region

	Burglary	Attempted burglary
Western Europe	2.3	2.8
New World	4.0	4.4
Countries in transition	3.6	3.5
Asia	2.3	1.5
Africa	8.3	7.3
Latin America	5.3	6.3

Table 2 reveals burglary rates for countries in transition. It can be noted that the highest rates for both completed and attempted burglary appear in Mongolia and Estonia. Latvia has high rates of attempted burglary but much lower rates for completed burglary while the opposite holds true for the Slovak Republic. The lowest household victimisation risks are found in Romania, Croatia and Belarus.

Table 2. Burglary and attempted burglary in countries in transition

	Burglary	Attempted burglary
Estonia	7.2	6.2
Poland	2.5	3.1
Czech Republic	4.0	3.0
Slovak Republic	6.5	2.2
Russia	2.5	4.0
Georgia	4.3	4.8
Slovenia	2.8	2.9
Latvia	2.9	6.2
Romania	1.1	2.2
Hungary	2.5	1.6
Yugoslavia	2.9	2.7
Albania	3.4	2.9
Macedonia	2.3	1.3
Croatia	0.9	1.4
Ukraine	3.6	4.5
Belarus	1.5	1.5
Bulgaria	5.8	5.7
Lithuania	5.5	3.9
Mongolia	9.0	5.9
Kyrgyzstan	4.0	3.8

Car related thefts

Before presenting the results relating to theft of and from cars, it is worth noting that vehicle ownership levels in countries in transition have increased in the past decade but are still, on average, lower than in urban developed world but higher than in the developing countries. In accordance with the opportunity theory, this fact itself would have increased the level of car related thefts. However, in countries in transition there is a modest negative correlation (-.3109) which indicates that the higher the ownership level the lower is the risk of owners having their cars stolen. A marked variation among countries in transition regarding the levels of vehicle ownership should be taken into consideration.

Table 3. Vehicle ownership rates in countries in transition

	Car ownership (1992-96)
Estonia	48.7
Poland	56.7
Czech Republic	65.8
Slovak Republic	60.7
Russia	37.3
Georgia	60.0
Slovenia	83.5
Latvia	46.0
Romania	45.5
Hungary	61.4
Yugoslavia	67.8
Albania	21.3
Macedonia	74.0
Croatia	71.0
Ukraine	33.9
Belarus	34.5
Bulgaria	64.0
Lithuania	56.3
Mongolia	26.2
Kyrgyzstan	43.5

Because of the above-mentioned variations, relative risks of car-related theft are more accurately based on owners only. This also provides for a greater reliability of data. A graphical analysis shows quite an interesting picture. There is a group of countries with low ownership rates and low risks of victimisation by car theft such as Albania, Mongolia, Belarus and Kyrgyzstan. Then there is a group of countries with high ownership rates but with low risks of victimisation such as Slovenia, Macedonia, Croatia, and Yugoslavia.

Figure 1. Thefts of and from cars by region

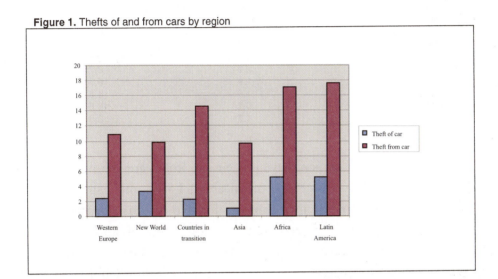

From a comparative perspective, theft from car is considerably higher in Latin America and Africa followed by countries in transition. The lowest rates are reported in Asia. As regards theft of cars, Africa and Latin America exhibit the highest rate followed by the New World. Countries in transition show similar rates of those of Western Europe.

Table 4. Theft of and from cars in countries in transition

	Theft of car	Theft from car
Estonia	4.2	24.3
Poland	2.7	15.7
Czech Republic	2.7	15.7
Slovakia	2.9	24.7
Russia	6.3	22.2
Georgia	2.6	16.8
Slovenia	0.4	9.4
Latvia	5.2	13.3
Romania	0.7	16.4
Hungary	3.0	11.5
Yugoslavia	2.0	13.7
Albania	1.0	22.9
Macedonia	0.6	9.9
Croatia	1.4	5.6
Ukraine	4.1	10.1
Belarus	2.0	8.7
Bulgaria	1.9	19.5
Lithuania	1.9	18.8
Mongolia	0.7	18.8
Kyrgyzstan	1.7	8.5

The risks of owners having their car stolen are the highest in Russia, followed by two Baltic urban areas, Latvia and Estonia, but also in Ukraine. Cars are usually stolen for two reasons: for joyriding (when they are usually recovered), or for extended appropriation including for personal use and resale. On average, the highest percentage of stolen cars are recovered in the New World and Western Europe while in Asia and Latin America more stolen cars are not recovered than those that are recovered. In countries in transition just over half of the stolen cars have been recovered. This, coupled with a trend towards more professional theft to do with demand for new and second-hand cars in Eastern and Central Europe (Liukkonen, 1997), suggests that there is a developed organised crime industry in car theft markets.

Obviously, there are marked variations in the stolen car recovery rates in countries in transition, ranging from as high as 93%

in Mongolia (but there are fewer cars and the market is geographically still removed from the mainstream car trafficking areas) to low stolen car recovery of only about a quarter of stolen cars in the Slovak Republic. The results are presented in Table 5.

Table 5. Recovery of stolen cars

	Stolen car recovered	Not recovered	Do not know
Estonia	71.8	28.2	
Poland	56.9	43.1	
Czech Republic	46.5	50.2	3.2
Slovak Republic	25.7	73.1	1.3
Russia	46.7	53.3	
Georgia	63.9	36.1	
Slovenia	48.5	51.5	
Latvia	51.9	46.4	1.8
Romania	100.0		
Hungary	45.8	53.4	0.8
Yugoslavia	49.1	50.9	
Albania	52.4	47.6	
Macedonia	79.4	20.6	
Croatia	44.5	53.6	1.8
Ukraine	70.5	26.6	2.9
Belarus	64.7	35.3	
Bulgaria	52.9	47.1	
Lithuania	56.1	43.9	
Mongolia	93.5	6.5	
Kyrgyzstan	30.7	66.1	3.2

As regards theft from vehicles (cars, vans and trucks) related to items left in the car, car equipment (e.g. car radios) or parts taken off cars, the highest risks are reported in the Slovak Republic, Bulgaria, Estonia, the Czech Republic, Georgia and Lithuania. Much lower rates are reported for Ukraine, Belarus and Kyrgyzstan.

Contact crimes

The summary measure of aggressive contact crime contains robbery, sexual assaults and assaults with force. Table 6 presents contact crime by world regions.

Table 6. Contact crime by world regions

	Robbery	Assault with force	Sexual assault
Western Europe	1.8	2.1	1.5
New World	1.5	2.9	1.7
Countries in transition	2.3	2.2	1.8
Asia	1.4	0.8	1.6
Africa	4.2	3.1	2.4
Latin America	8.1	2.7	5.0

Latin America and Africa exhibit the highest rates for contact crime while Asia shows the lowest rates. As regards countries in transition, they rank third in terms of robbery and sexual assault and fourth in terms of assault with force.

Table 7. Contact crime in countries in transition

	Robbery	Assault with force	Sexual assault
Estonia	4.9	4.0	2.2
Poland	2.2	2.8	2.1
Czech Republic	1.1	1.9	4.3
Slovak Republic	1.2	0.3	0.2
Russia	3.8	2.8	2.5
Georgia	3.8	1.6	1.8
Slovenia	1.1	1.8	2.5
Latvia	3.4	1.4	0.4
Romania	1.0	4.3	1.1
Hungary	0.7	0.6	0.0
Yugoslavia	1.1	2.9	2.1
Albania	1.4	0.8	2.9
Macedonia	1.1	1.3	0.5
Croatia	0.8	1.9	1.0
Ukraine	5.7	2.2	1.7
Belarus	2.0	2.0	1.5
Bulgaria	3.1	2.5	1.0
Lithuania	2.0	1.9	1.0
Mongolia	3.6	3.7	1.1
Kyrgyzstan	1.6	3.1	1.9

Risks of robbery were highest in Ukraine, Estonia, Russia, Georgia, Mongolia and Latvia; Estonia and Mongolia also show high risks for assault with force, as do Romania and Kyrgyzstan and, to a somewhat lesser degree, Yugoslavia, Russia, Poland and Bulgaria. As regards sexual assault (defined as incidents described by victims as rape, attempted rape or indecent assault) the Czech Republic shows the highest risk followed by Albania, Russia, Slovenia, Estonia, Poland and Yugoslavia.

Other crime

This group of crimes comprises car vandalism, theft of motorcycles and bicycles, theft of personal property, offensive sexual behaviour and threats. While this group consists of rather different crimes, these are pooled together insofar as they are typically perceived as not very serious crimes. Figure 2 presents a regional view.

Figure 2. Other crime by world regions

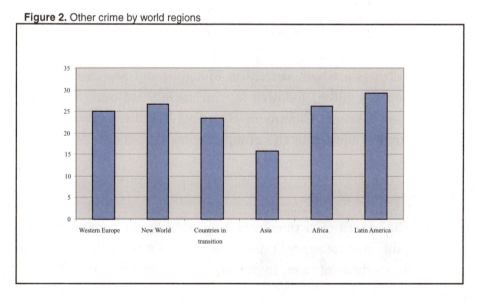

Latin America, Africa and the New World show the highest risks for this group of crime while Asia shows the lowest. Countries in transition and Western Europe exhibit similar levels of risk for other crime.

Table 8. Other crime in countries in transition

	Other crime
Estonia	27.4
Poland	26.5
Czech Republic	25.4
Slovak Republic	28.7
Russia	25.1
Georgia	19.4
Slovenia	29.1
Latvia	20.8
Romania	22.3
Hungary	15.6
Yugoslavia	22.8
Albania	22.3
Macedonia	15.2
Croatia	16.3
Ukraine	27.7
Belarus	16.3
Bulgaria	24.6
Lithuania	21.4
Mongolia	30.2
Kyrgyzstan	18.5

Taken as a whole, citizens in Mongolia and Slovenia were at the highest risk (30%) followed by citizens in the Slovak Republic, Estonia and Ukraine. Citizens in Hungary, Macedonia, Belarus and Croatia are less affected by this group of crime.

Country profiles of crime

The pattern of victimisation is reflected by the composition of crime in different countries. Table 9 summarises some main points. In addition to theft of and from cars, car vandalism, bicycle and motorcycle theft, and theft of personal property a category of other personal crime (robbery, assaults/threats, sexual offences) was also included.

Table 9: Profile of crime by countries in transition (% of all offences: total =100%)

	Theft of and from cars	Car vandalism	Bicycle and motorcycle theft	Burglary and attempts	Theft of personal property	Other personal crime*
Estonia	24	14	7	18	12	25
Poland	20	21	7	12	18	21
Czech Republic	25	11	10	14	29	12
Slovak Republic	34	22	8	13	17	7
Russia	22	15	5	12	22	24
Georgia	32	2	3	20	20	22
Slovenia	18	27	8	12	12	23
Latvia	20	10	4	20	30	17
Romania	21	11	1	9	31	27
Hungary	28	32	6	10	16	7
Yugoslavia	32	15	2	11	18	22
Albania	18	3	20	15	22	21
Macedonia	34	20	4	11	18	14
Croatia	16	30	4	8	17	25
Ukraine	9	9	3	16	40	24
Belarus	15	14	6	13	23	28
Bulgaria	34	15	2	18	16	15
Lithuania	30	15	3	17	20	16
Mongolia	10	5	3	23	42	18
Kyrgyzstan	12	7	5	19	31	26

* Other personal crime: robbery, assaults/threats, and sexual offences.

Theft involving cars

Around one third of crimes reported in the ICVS in Bulgaria, Macedonia, the Slovak Republic, Yugoslavia, Georgia and Lithuania involve theft of and from cars. They accounted for the smallest amount of the crime totals in Ukraine and Mongolia.

Car vandalism

Between a quarter and a third of crime totals in Hungary, Croatia and Slovenia are composed of car vandalism while it represents a very small portion of crime totals in Georgia and Albania.

Theft of bicycles and motorcycles

On average, this group participates the least in crime totals with the exception of Albania.

Burglary

The participation of burglary (completed and attempted) in crime totals of countries in transition is more substantial than for industrialised countries (Mayhew and van Dijk, 1997). In Mongolia, Slovenia, Latvia, Kyrgyzstan, Bulgaria and Poland burglary accounts for some 20% of crime totals; it represents less than 10% of the crime totals only in Romania and Croatia.

Theft of personal property

This ranges from 42% and 40% respectively in Mongolia and Ukraine to 12% in Estonia and Slovenia.

Other personal crimes

This group consists of contact crime and threats, and offensive sexual behaviour and account for a bit less than one quarter of crime incidents. The highest figures are for Belarus, Kyrgyzstan and Estonia while the lowest are for Hungary and the Slovak Republic.

Trends in crime

As regards the crime trends in countries in transition, only six out of twenty countries participated both in the 1992 and 1996 sweeps of the ICVS (Poland, Estonia, Russia, Georgia, Slovenia and the Czech Republic). In the 1992 ICVS, data were collected for the whole of the former Czechoslovakia but then after the dismemberment of the Federation and the creation of two independent countries (the Czech Republic and the Slovak Republic) only data from the Czech part of the 1992 ICVS and the Czech Republic of the 1996 ICVS are used for trend analysis.[2]

Table 10. Trends in 1992-96 for selected crimes in countries in transition

	Car theft			Burglary			Personal theft			Robbery			Assault		
	1992	1996	Diff.	1992	1996	Diff.	1992	1996	Diff.	1992	1996	Diff.	1992	1996	Diff.
Estonia	3.3	5.0	1.8	8.4	5.8	-2.6	12.0	6.7	-5.3	4.4	5.4	1.0	7.5	7.5	0.0
Poland	1.7	2.9	1.1	2.6	2.5	-0.1	13.7	7.0	-6.7	2.5	2.0	-0.5	5.7	4.5	-1.2
Czech Rep.	1.3	3.7	2.4	6.2	3.0	-3.2	10.3	14.0	3.7	0.4	1.5	1.1	2.7	3.4	0.7
Russia	2.8	4.5	1.7	1.8	3.2	1.4	10.8	12.7	1.9	3.4	4.2	0.8	4.9	5.7	0.8
Georgia	5.6	2.6	-3.0	2.5	4.3	1.8	3.5	8.8	5.3	1.6	3.2	1.6	0.5	3.7	3.2
Slovenia	0.4	0.2	-0.1	1.7	3.9	2.2	4.1	6.5	2.4	0.2	1.9	1.7	1.7	6.2	4.5

Car theft

Car theft increased in four countries (Estonia, Poland, the Czech Republic and Russia) while it decreased in Georgia and, to a lesser degree, in Slovenia.

Burglary

Burglary decreased in Estonia, the Czech Republic and slightly in Poland while it increased in Russia, Georgia and Slovenia.

Personal theft

Personal theft increased in four out of six countries but substantially decreased in Estonia and Poland.

Robbery

Robbery increased in five countries but slightly decreased in Poland.

---

2   *The Slovak data base disaggregated from the 1992 Czechoslovakia Survey was too small to allow for trend analysis.*

Assault

Assault increased in five countries with the exception of Poland.

The above data reveal that, on average, there was an increase in crime in the period 1992-96, particularly for contact crime (represented by robbery and assault) and personal theft. Trends in car theft and burglary were split between an increase in three countries (Estonia, Poland and the Czech Republic) and a decrease in another countries (Russia, Georgia and Slovenia) as regards car theft, and in the opposite direction as regards burglary (for the same countries).

References

Liukkonen, M. (1997). *Motor Vehicle Theft in Europe: International Cooperation in the Prevention and Control of the Theft of and Illicit Trafficking in Motor Vehicles.* HEUNI: HEUNI Papers.

Mayhew, P. and van Dijk, J.J. (1997). *Criminal Victimisation in Eleven Industrialised Countries.* The Hague: WODC.

CHAPTER 4

Corruption in Public Administration and Consumer Fraud

This chapter discusses findings related to street level corruption and consumer fraud. Although conventional, these "crimes" are somewhat different from other conventional crimes to do with property and violence. The interest lies in exploring common victimisation experiences related to public administration and the provision of goods and services in the market. Corruption and consumer fraud are therefore more indicators of good governance and consumer protection than of public safety.

Corruption is an ubiquitous and perennial phenomenon. It might be said without running a high risk of exaggeration, that corruption runs throughout human political history. It finds the most fruitful grounds in situations in which there are unfettered discretionary decision-making powers without adequate political, ethical and legal frameworks and measures to ensure accountability and transparency. It is very much linked to public office and authority discretion to decide on allocation of resources and/or issuance of public acts and documents, enforcement of administrative regulations and laws, control over the quality of goods and services, and facilitation of financial and legal transactions; in other words, all the necessary action to enable the management of both public and private affairs.

The concept of corruption has become multifaceted. It not only is the *sine qua non* of sustained organised crime and money laundering but also taints "civil" relations as in the case of "facilitation payments", issuance of licences and the usual ways "to get things done." The concept of corruption includes a number of transactions ranging from "simple bribery" of and by public officials, through abuse of office, to business corruption and corruption involving the financial and political centres of power. There are different criteria for defining corruption (e.g. public interest; public opinion; market perspective), the most diffused being corruption in public administration.

One of the major common difficulties, above and beyond definition and measurement issues, is related to the fact that corruption - as most other crimes - lends itself to being known only if reported and reacted upon. Since it involves a "clandestine and confidential" relationship it is no surprise that only a small portion of corruption is known and then reacted upon. More often than not, corruption is either a process of transactions and thus of a certain duration for the parties involved, or an individual corrupt transaction in a wider transactional context in which some transactions are illegal while others are perfectly legal. In addition, some societies may be more tolerant towards corruption of public officials, which is often considered and justified as being part of traditional folklore in the relationship between public officials and citizens.

Analysis of the ICVS results on bribery

The International Crime Victim Survey has an advantage over the other sources of information on corruption in that it provides for a measurement of the magnitude based on the direct experience of citizens and targets it to public officials. In other words, it attempts to capture the magnitude of bribery by public officials, which is probably the most diffused and most conventional form of corruption.[1] Despite a number of limits of victim surveys, including the ICVS (Zvekic, 1996), it appears that the latter offers better measures of corruption than other surveys or official criminal justice statistics (Woltring and Shinkai, 1996).

The item of corruption was included for the first time in the second sweep of the ICVS and then it was administered only in the developing countries and countries in transition. Pilots carried out in three industrialised countries revealed at the time that it was a rare event and thus corruption was not included in the questionnaire administered in the industrialised world. However, the period between the second and third sweeps of the ICVS witnessed the disclosure of a number of serious cases of corruption in some industrialised countries, which indicated that it would be worth including the corruption item for all countries participating in the

---

1   "In some areas there is a problem of corruption among government or public officials. During (last year) has any government official, for instance a customs officer, police officer or inspector in your country, asked you or expected you to pay a bribe for his service?" Following this question the respondents were asked to identify the category of public official, and whether it was reported to the police (public prosecutor) or other public or private agency.

ICVS. Another reason was comparative and political: the ICVS should provide for international comparison and the exclusion of an item in some countries would limit such an objective. On the other hand, it was felt that maintaining the corruption item for the developing world and countries in transition only would be prejudicial and politically unacceptable. Therefore, the third sweep of the ICVS included a corruption question for all participating sites.

An analysis of the results of the ICVS clearly reveals that bribery of public officials is, in descending order, more diffused in the developing world, followed by countries in transition, and was negligible in the industrialised world.

Table 1. Bribery of public officials: one-year prevalence rates

Developing world	17.6
Countries in transition	12.8
Industrialised world	1.0

This is further supported by an analysis of the overall rates of crime types dealt with by the ICVS on a regional level. Indeed, in both sweeps of the ICVS, corruption was - together with consumer fraud - the most common form of victimisation of citizens in the developing world and countries in transition. On average, bribery is - second to consumer fraud - the most diffused form of victimisation of citizens in all but the industrialised world.

Table 2. One-year prevalence rates for bribery by regions

Western Europe	1.0
New World	0.9
Countries in transition	12.8
Asia	16.6
Africa	15.0
Latin America	19.5

48

The results presented above reveal that corruption in public administration is most diffused in Latin America, followed by Asia and Africa. This supports the previously mentioned findings that it is the public administration in the developing countries and countries in transition that is more receptive to challenges of corruption. Consequently, the citizens in those parts of the world are at a higher risk of being victimised by corrupt public administration. Obviously, it should be noted that corruption is a process and a relationship in which the citizens are involved in different ways but most frequently in two of them. First, in order to effect their legitimate rights and interests which, due to the malfunctioning of the public administration and/or complexity of regulation, they are not able to realise through normal channels and on time. Second, to realise their specific interests, which may not be legitimate, they tend to utilise corruptible public administration.

Table 3. Countries in transition

Albania	13.8
Belarus	12.0
Bulgaria	19.1
Czech Republic	8.8
Croatia	15.2
Estonia	3.8
Georgia	29.9
Hungary	3.9
Kyrgyzstan	21.3
Latvia	14.0
Lithuania	13.4
Macedonia	7.7
Mongolia	5.1
Poland	7.4
Romania	11.9
Russia	18.7
Slovak Republic	13.9
Slovenia	1.5
Ukraine	12.6
Yugoslavia	17.4

With respect to other regions, bribery in countries in transition ranks as the third most common form of victimisation after consumer fraud and theft from car/vandalism. Sites from the Commonwealth of Independent States, such as Tbilisi (Georgia), Bishkek and Osh (Kyrgyzstan) and Moscow (Russia) exhibit the highest levels, but also Belgrade (F.R. of Yugoslavia), Riga (Latvia), Tirana (Albania) and Kiev (Ukraine). The lowest levels of bribery are recorded for Budapest (Hungary), urban Estonia and Ljubljana (Slovenia). There appears to be a certain pattern indicating that the rates of corruption in public administration are lower (on average) in those countries in transition that have reached notable levels of change of both a political and economic character (Hungary, Poland, the Czech Republic, Estonia) and most probably have improved on their public administration, too. On the other hand, high levels of corruption in public administration are noted in the countries in which the process of transition was slower (e.g. a number of former republics of the Soviet Union and the former Yugoslavia).

While possible explanations cover a range of factors, including specific cultural ones, these findings do indicate that it is most likely that street level corruption by public officials has to do with the standards of public administration, on the one hand, and with the overall position of citizens, on the other. Bribery by public officials is therefore less likely in societies in which the public administration has a more developed service orientation, is better paid and trained, and has both internal and external control mechanisms over legality and efficiency; in other words, in which accountability and transparency are at a higher stake and in which the culture of public administration is that of a service to citizens rather than that of exercising power over citizens. However, the influence of cultural patterns consisting in making gifts as well as the *tout court* low level of confidence by citizenry towards public administration should be taken into full consideration.

It appears, on the basis of different sources of information, that bribery as a "way of getting things done" is present both in the business and public administration sectors in countries in transition. A high statistical correlation tends to indicate that this might be the case although the evidence is not decisive.[2] It might be hypothesised that high street level corruption indicates the presence of serious forms of corruption as well. However, low street level corruption does not indicate the absence of serious forms of corruption. We often get to know about serious forms of corruption when a particular political and situational context exists in which judicial and other authorities initiate prosecution of corruption cases. We learn of these from the mass media, which also inform about the course and direction of the fight against corruption. Since the influence of the mass media is stronger in the industrialised world, we tend to know more about more serious cases of corruption taking place in the industrialised countries. In developing countries quite often corruption cases are disclosed only after or during the course of changing political rulers. In countries in transition, the democratisation of the mass media has contributed enormously to disclosures of corruption both in public administration as well as among the financial and political centres of power. However, the process of privatisation has also opened up new opportunities for corruption, including the nexuses involving public administration, financial and political centres of power and organised crime. Corruption transparency goes hand in hand with democracy, legal and financial certainty and transparency as well as the culture of

---

2   *The Spearman correlation coefficient of 882 (N=20; p<0.001) between the Transparency International Corruption Index and the results of the ICVS.*

public responsibility and accountability and the means to provide for it.

On average, corruption cases are less reported than most other crimes dealt with by the ICVS. The level of reported corruption is higher in the New World countries than in the countries in transition and developing countries. The inverse relationship between the magnitude of experienced corruption and the volume reported to the police is particularly evident in Latin America, Africa and countries in transition. This inverse relationship also holds true at the country level. For example, the lowest percentage of corruption cases reported to the police is in Kampala which has the highest level of corruption experienced by its citizens. There is an opposite situation in Asia where Manila exhibits the lowest level of corruption and the highest reporting rate.

As regards countries in transition, their average reporting level for bribery is the lowest from the regional comparative perspective. Although the overall relationship between the magnitude of corruption and its reporting to the police is similar to other regions, there are more pronounced variations. Nevertheless, the fact remains that the overall level of reporting bribery in countries in transition is lower. A possible explanation for this might be that a number of cases are reported to public prosecutors' offices which, in many countries in transition, are in charge of corruption. Bribery may be reported to other public or private agencies but it appears that in many countries these are not readily available. Nevertheless, the pattern of reporting to other agencies is similar to that of reporting to the police. There is more reporting in industrialised countries than in the developing world and the least in countries in transition.

Reporting of bribery, as noted above, has one of the lowest reporting levels from among crimes dealt with by the ICVS. In all likelihood, this has to do with the type of public officials involved in bribery and the relationship between citizens and public administration.

Table 4. Type of public official involved in bribery by regions

	Government official	Customs officer	Police officer	Inspector	Other	Don't know
Western Europe	39.9	20.3	18.7	0.0	17.0	4.2
New World	0.0	33.5	51.5	0.0	15.0	0.0
Countries in transition	25.9	16.7	29.9	12.3	13.8	1.4
Asia	44.8	3.3	39.2	3.6	9.1	0.0
Africa	27.1	14.5	31.8	8.0	18.6	0.0
Latin America	13.0	9.8	47.4	19.8	9.6	0.4

Table 5. Type of public officials involved in bribery in countries in transition

	Government official	Customs officer	Police officer	Inspector	Other	Do not know
Estonia	6.3	6.3	28.1	12.5	18.8	28.1
Poland	25.0	16.9	27.0	22.0	9.1	0.0
Czech Republic	31.3	6.5	26.8	24.1	11.3	0.0
Slovak Republic	25.4	5.5	32.5	27.6	9.0	0.0
Russia	16.1	5.7	52.2	8.2	17.8	0.0
Georgia	11.5	32.3	30.1	25.3	0.8	0.0
Slovenia	13.8	37.2	19.3	5.4	24.3	0.0
Latvia	37.4	22.3	12.3	16.5	10.4	1.1
Romania	56.8	6.9	13.8	6.6	15.8	0.0
Hungary	12.8	21.2	34.6	0.0	31.4	0.0
Yugoslavia	26.8	21.2	40.5	4.3	7.2	0.0
Albania	36.2	13.3	8.1	15.4	26.3	0.7
Macedonia	18.7	32.5	9.5	6.5	30.6	2.2
Croatia	20.6	10.3	41.6	4.3	17.2	6.0
Ukraine	23.4	12.6	25.7	8.6	28.6	1.1
Belarus	33.1	16.3	20.1	9.1	18.6	2.8
Bulgaria	4.6	15.0	54.2	6.0	19.2	0.9
Lithuania	20.6	21.1	32.5	6.9	18.9	0.0
Mongolia	25.3	37.7	15.1	13.0	8.9	0.0
Kyrgyzstan	37.7	19.3	23.1	12.6	3.5	3.7

From among the various public officials, police officers appear to be the category most involved in bribery, particularly in Latin

America and the New World. In Asia and in countries in transition, police officers are second to government officials. Customs officers rank high on the bribery-prone scale, particularly in Africa, countries in transition and in the New World, while inspectors' involvement is high in Latin America and in countries in transition. The level of reporting does not vary by the type of public official involved in bribery. Custom officers in Asia and police officers in the New World are the most reported categories among the few cases reported at all.

Among the public officials involved in corruption in countries in transition the most frequently reported are police officers, particularly in Russia, Bulgaria, Croatia, Yugoslavia, Hungary, Lithuania, the Slovak Republic and Georgia. Customs officers are most often involved in bribery in Slovenia, Macedonia, Mongolia and Georgia. Government officials are bribery prone especially in Romania, Kyrgyzstan, Latvia, Albania and Belarus.

Table 6. Corruption perceived and experienced according to the International Commercial Crime Survey, 1994*

	Corruption very common or fairly common %	Victimisation experienced %
Australia	-	1.0
Netherlands	10.9	2.4
Germany	14.7	3.2
France	1.4	4.8
Switzerland	2.8	3.6
Italy	15.4	1.5
UK	7.4	1.8
South Africa	-	
Hungary	16.4	3.0
Czech Republic	34.1	4.7

* This table is constructed by using a combination of data from Tables 1 and 3 presented in van Dijk and Terlouw (1996).

An attempt toward measuring perceptions and victimisation experienced by retailers and small business was undertaken in 1994 by the first International Commercial Crime Survey (ICCS) conducted in seven industrialised countries, two Eastern-Central European countries and one developing country on samples of businesses extracted from Commerce Chambers lists (van Dijk and Terlouw, 1996). A series of questions on corruption were included, starting from the perception of how common corruption was in the country and then moving to actual experiences of the respondents.[3]

Table 6 reveals that retailers, particularly in the Czech Republic (34%) and in Hungary (16%) but also in Italy and Germany (15%), believe that quite a lot of corruption occurs in their sector. Although the level of experienced victimisation by corruption is much lower than the perceived one, it should be noted that the rank orders of the two measures of corruption match fairly well, although in France and Switzerland the level of experienced corruption outstrips that of perceived diffusion of corruption. Yet there is a clear gap between average levels of experienced and perceived corruption in Western Europe retail trade (2.88% and 8.76% respectively), on the one hand, and the levels in Central and Eastern European countries (3.85% and 25.25% respectively), on the other. Although these data are limited by the size of the sample, particularly for Central and Eastern Europe,

---

3   The respondents were asked the following question first: "I would now like to ask you about corruption. By corruption I mean: bribing employees or companies; extorting money from a company; obtaining protection money; threats of product contamination; bribery or extortion by government officials; and it includes also attempts to act like that. Do you believe such practices are common in your line of business? Are they very common, fairly common, not very common or not common at all?". Then the interviewer continued with the following question: "Did anyone try to bribe you, your employees, or obtain bribes from the company, or extort money from your company in relation to its activities at these premises? This includes trying to obtain protection money or threats of product contamination. Bribery or extortion by government officials is also included".

they support the findings related to citizens' experience of corruption. In other words, both corruption of public administration and that of the business sector are higher in countries in transition, even taking into account the fact that the Czech Republic and Hungary are among the most advanced countries in transition in terms of political, economic and public administration reforms, and with relatively modest levels of corruption of public administration as reported by the ICVS.

Consumer fraud

Together with corruption, consumer fraud is one of the most common forms of citizens' victimisation across the board. In the ICVS this type of victimisation regarded a number of ways in which citizens were cheated in the quantity and quality of goods attained and services received.[4]

Table 7. Consumer fraud by regions

Western Europe	12.7
New World	8.0
Countries in transition	39.7
Asia	26.1
Africa	38.9
Latin America	24.6

---

4   *The respondents were asked the following question: "Last year, were you the victim of a consumer fraud? In other words, has someone when selling something to you or delivering a service cheated you in terms of quantity or quality of the goods/services?". Furthermore, the respondents were asked "How did this fraud take place (last time)? Was it to do with: construction or repair work; work done by garage; a hotel, restaurant or pub: a shop of some sort" and then whether it was reported to the police or some other public or private agency.*

Similarly to corruption, consumer fraud is more experienced in the developing world and countries in transition than in the industrialised world, both Old and New. The lowest rate of consumer fraud is found in the New World while the highest is in Africa and in countries in transition. There are great variations between countries in Africa, ranging from 88% and 60% in Tanzania and Tunisia to 5% in South Africa.

Table 8. Consumer fraud in countries in transition

Albania	12.4
Belarus	40.6
Bulgaria	55.0
Czech Republic	55.3
Croatia	33.8
Estonia	34.2
Georgia	53.1
Hungary	34.5
Kyrgyzstan	71.0
Latvia	33.3
Lithuania	32.7
Macedonia	31.2
Mongolia	25.5
Poland	18.1
Romania	39.2
Russia	51.5
Slovak Republic	35.4
Slovenia	21.6
Ukraine	67.6
Yugoslavia	49.6

Similarly, in countries in transition the highest rates are recorded in countries in which, by many parameters, the market economy is still nascent such as Kyrgyzstan, Ukraine, F.R. Yugoslavia and Georgia or where adequate regulatory mechanisms are not developed or are difficult to enforce (Russia, Bulgaria, the Czech Republic). This tells a lot about the protection of citizens as consumers as well as about the standard quality of goods and services. Most probably, the introduction of the free market and private service in the retail sectors in these countries without adequate regulation and well developed ethical standards and care regarding consumer satisfaction have influenced such a state of affairs.

The afore-mentioned International Commercial Crime Survey (van Dijk and Terlouw, 1996) also provides information on fraud in the business sector (retail trade). Table 9 presents data related to fraud by inside personnel and by outsiders.

Table 9. Fraud in the business sector (retail trade), ICCS, 1996

	Fraud by personnel %	Fraud by outsiders %
Netherlands	3.0	12.6
Germany	3.1	27.6
France	1.3	42.3
Switzerland	1.3	13.6
Czech Republic	6.0	21.2
UK	2.5	21.0
Hungary	2.9	11.2
Italy	1.6	24.7
Australia	1.7	19.7

The business sector was much more victimised by fraud by outsiders rather than by its own personnel. As for the former, the most exposed were the retail trade enterprises in France, Italy, Switzerland and the Czech Republic, while insider fraud was most frequent in the Czech Republic, followed by Germany, the Netherlands and Hungary. While the Czech Republic ranks high on both fraud types, Hungary is low on fraud committed by outsiders. Although data cannot be taken as representative for the group of countries in transition, still both on business fraud and on citizens' victimisation by fraud, the Czech Republic ranks high. As noted, it ranks first and fourth as regards business fraud (insiders and outsiders respectively) and third on consumer fraud experienced by citizens-consumers. Hungary, for all three means of fraud is in the upper middle part of the fraud scale. Thus, there is quite a high level of congruence among the three measures of fraud in countries in transition, supporting the finding that it is indeed one of the most common forms of victimisation experienced in countries in transition by the citizens-consumers as well as by businesses.

As regards type of fraud, the ICVS respondents were asked to identify the premises or services for which they felt they were is some way cheated the last time. Across the board (with the exception of the New World), citizens are mostly subject to cheating while purchasing goods at shops; this holds true for Western Europe (although the "others" category also figures substantially), for the developing world and for countries in transition. On average, between 10% and 40% of the victims pointed out that they were cheated when purchasing goods followed by "cheats" related to construction work and repairs. However, it should be noted that citizens from the developing world and countries in transition were more often subject to consumer fraud related to the purchase of goods than those in the industrialised world.

Table 10. Type of consumer fraud by regions

	Construction/ repair	Car garage	Hotel	Shop	Other
Western Europe	12.6	4.3	4.5	57.6	20.9
New World	14.7	7.5	0.5	9.8	66.7
Countries in transition	3.8	4.1	7.0	63.7	16.6
Asia	5.8	5.5	3.4	62.0	23.3
Africa	16.1	5.9	5.6	50.5	22.0
Latin America	16.6	6.9	7.2	46.7	22.0

Only a few report consumer fraud to the police. With some exceptions, something like 95% of consumer fraud was not reported to the police or to any other public or private agency. However, levels of reporting to other private or public agencies do differ to some extent. On average, in the industrialised world there appear to be more non-police agencies to which citizens can report consumer fraud. This is particularly the case in the UK, USA and Canada. For example, 18% and 24% of consumer fraud is reported in Western Europe and the New World to agencies other than the police. Also in Latin America some 14% of consumer fraud is reported to other agencies. Consumer protection is much more developed and organised in the industrialised world and in particular in the New World. Efforts towards the standardisation of the quality of goods and services, the development of appropriate commercial ethics, including an interest in durable relations and customers' satisfaction, the creation of consumer protection associations as well as the further stabilisation of markets are more viable methods for reducing consumer fraud.

Table 11. Type of consumer fraud in countries in transition, 1996

	Construction/ repair	Car garage	Hotel	Shop	Other
Estonia	0.8	0.8	1.2	88.4	7.6
Poland	3.9	5.3	6.3	71.4	13.1
Czech Republic	8.5	7.8	21.8	56.9	3.9
Slovak Republic	2.9	4.8	33.5	55.8	2.6
Russia	2.1	2.9	0.6	74.5	19.5
Georgia	2.6	3.9	6.8	49.4	37.0
Slovenia	8.3	3.4	2.5	59.3	25.5
Latvia	4.0	8.3	6.5	71.5	7.1
Romania	2.2	5.4	7.2	50.3	34.0
Hungary	6.3	4.4	1.6	73.6	13.7
Yugoslavia	7.5	5.5	6.2	44.8	35.9
Albania	9.1	0.8	5.1	67.3	17.7
Macedonia	2.3	11.6	7.1	75.0	2.9
Croatia	6.8	7.2	7.2	73.8	4.7
Ukraine	1.0	1.5	1.1	26.5	19.3
Belarus	3.5	2.3	4.3	67.1	22.4
Bulgaria	2.9	3.9	6.1	82.8	4.1
Lithuania	2.2	4.5	3.1	60.1	29.4
Mongolia	0.7	0.4	2.0	36.4	60.5
Kyrgyzstan	3.4	1.9	6.4	86.4	1.9

References

Shinkai, H. (Ed.) (1997). 'Combating corruption in Central and Eastern Europe'. UNICRI series *Issues & Reports*, No.10.

Van Dijk, J.J.M. and Terlouw, G.J. (1996). 'An international perspective of the business community as victims of fraud and crime'. *Security Journal*, 7.

Woltring, H. and Shinkai, H. (1996). 'Corruption: Approaches towards the analysis in the international context'. *Social Defence, Corruption, Protection of Public Administration and the Independence of Justice*. Proceedings of the XIIIth International Congress on Social Defence. Lecce, Italy, 28-30 November 1996. Harwood Academic Publishers (in print).

Zvekic, U. (1996). 'International Crime Victim Survey: comparative advantages and disadvantages'. *International Criminal Justice Review*, Vol. 6.

CHAPTER 5

Citizens and Police:
Confidence Building in the Process of Democratisation

Policing is at the beginning of the criminal justice system. Policing encompasses the routine provision of administrative services to citizens, patrolling, criminal investigation, recovery of stolen property, and bringing suspects to justice; it also encourages certain punitive functions such as detention and administration of fines. Obviously, the police have different functions in different criminal justice systems. Yet in most countries policing is a mixture of preventive, administrative and repressive functions.

The police are usually the first criminal justice agency with which citizens come into contact, and they will shape opinions about the justice system as a whole. No other agency of justice is under such continuous public scrutiny and the object of such frequent political debate regarding powers of control, issues of privacy, crime prevention, and control priorities. Often, the real or perceived failure of the police to meet real or perceived community interests leads to the development of alternative policing styles (Findlay and Zvekic, 1993).

This evaluative process is based either on direct experience or on expectations as to what should be done. It is almost always an intrinsic interplay between experiences and expectations. Experience is not the exclusive domain of crime victims. Rather, experience of the police comes mainly from routine contacts with them as they administer public services: daily observation of policing in the local area, mass media reports about policing activities, or knowledge of the policing experiences of family members, friends and neighbours. Obviously, criminal victimisation itself gives more opportunity for informed evaluation, though the particular position of the victim may result in biased generalisations.

Reporting to the police

The "police crime story" is the amount and type of crime known to them. It will differ from the "real crime story" depending on citizens' propensity to inform the police about crime. To this reported crime, the police can add crimes detected by them but not reported, and they can deduct some criminal activities which do not figure in the "police crime story" because of specific investigative, technical, procedural, social and political reasons. There are, however, important variations across countries as to the volume and type of crime known to the police and admitted into police administrative records. The ICVS[1] provides considerable information as to

1   For the results of the 1992-94 ICVS related to policing, see Zvekic (1997).

differences across countries in crimes experienced by victims, and those reported to the police. It does not, however, provide information on the way in which reported crimes are officially admitted into police records.

Not surprisingly, the propensity to report to the police depends heavily on the seriousness of the crime, whether tangible or intangible. However, reporting is also influenced by other factors: previous personal experiences of reporting; other acquired experience with, or attitudes to the police; expectations; factors related to the particular victimisation experience in hand; the existence of alternative ways of dealing with this; the relationship with the offender; and the "privacy" of the issue.

Crime reporting, as mentioned above, differs according to the crime in question. It is evident that car theft is more reported than any other crime, while sexual incidents, corruption and consumer fraud are, on average, the least reported. However, reporting rates also differ from country to country as well as depending on the developmental level. It is also claimed that the reporting rates have to do with the crime level in the society irrespective of the above-mentioned factors or as a baseline from which other factors influence the levels of reporting.

For illustrative purposes, reporting rates for burglary, robbery and assault based on all sweeps of the ICVS are presented in Table 1.

Among the three crimes, the highest reporting level is for burglary followed by robbery. Less than one third of the victims of assault reported it to the police. For all three crimes the highest reporting levels are in the industrialised world, both Old and New. From among the group of non-industrialised countries, burglary is reported the most in countries in transition and in Africa, and the least in Asia; while from among the non-industrialised group less than one third of the victims reported assault and somewhat more than a third reported robbery to the police. Therefore, in terms of the "reporting ranks" countries in transition rank third on burglary, fifth on robbery and fourth on assault. There is then a clear difference in reporting levels between, on the one hand, the industrialised world and, on the other, the rest of the world.

Table 1. Percentage of burglary, robbery and assault reported to the police in six global regions, 1989, 1992 and 1996 ICVS (1 year)

	Burglary	Robbery	Assault
Western Europe	79.6	45.5	28.5
New World	85.3	75.9	45.3
Countries in transition	63.2	25.1	20.4
Asia	40.8	33.3	31.0
Africa	57.7	33.5	20.4
Latin America	44.1	20.7	23.6
Total	61.8	39.0	28.2

Comparing the two data sets (victimisation rates [Chapter 3] and reporting rates) it becomes clear that the highest level of correspondence between the victimisation and reporting rates for all three crime types is found in Asia. From a comparative perspective, Asia has both the lowest victimisation as well as the lowest reporting rates. On the other hand, the highest reporting rates of the New World do not correspond to the victimisation levels reported for the New World. Generally speaking, it appears that the reporting levels do not reflect the victimisation levels. This seems to support the hypothesis that the victimisation level is not the most important factor in conditioning the reporting practice and that it cannot be considered even a solid baseline for predicting propensity to report to the police. High crime does not automatically and necessarily lead to high disclosures of crime. Other factors appear to have more weight on the propensity to report to the police.

It is more difficult to reach such oversweeping generalisations if one looks at the regional and/or country level details.

Table 2. Reporting rates in countries in transition: burglary, robbery and assault, 1989, 1992 and 1996 - by country

	Burglary	Robbery	Assault
Albania	47.4	22.9	20.0
Belarus	47.1	26.2	19.5
Bulgaria	62.8	37.1	20.3
Croatia	61.4	30.1	25.5
Czech Republic	84.1	74.7	27.2
Estonia	66.5	31.0	16.5
Georgia	51.7	27.4	68.9
Hungary	78.9	45.8	18.1
Kyrgyzstan	59.4	27.4	13.6
Latvia	74.4	25.2	16.0
Lithuania	58.3	43.7	24.5
Macedonia	64.8	40.7	33.0
Mongolia	69.4	33.2	21.3
Poland	57.7	29.9	26.9
Romania	86.3	30.9	23.0
Russia	62.5	21.1	21.2
Slovak Republic	61.8	44.4	33.3
Slovenia	67.1	27.2	28.4
Ukraine	49.8	32.2	20.7
Yugoslavia	70.5	36.9	28.6

From among the 20 countries in transition, most of them (12) exhibit high reporting rates for burglary; four very high rates (> 75) and three low reporting rates (< 50). High burglary reporting countries are Romania, the Czech Republic, Hungary and Latvia. As regards the reporting of robbery, it averages half of the reporting rates for burglary with the Czech Republic, having the highest rate followed by Hungary, the Slovak Republic, Lithuania and Macedonia. The lowest reporting rates are found in Russia and Albania. As noted above, assault is the least reported crime type from among those analysed herewith. In Georgia, assault is very frequently reported to the police (69) and it is also relatively frequently reported in the Slovak Republic, Macedonia, Yugoslavia and the Czech Republic. It is least reported in Estonia, Latvia, Albania and Belarus.

As noted above, it is difficult to establish a clear correspondence pattern between the victimisation experience and reporting practice, which further supports the earlier mentioned observations regarding the relationship between crime occurrence and crime disclosure.

Several countries participated in both sweeps of the ICVS, as mentioned above. As regards burglary, the most significant changes in terms of more burglaries being reported to the police are found in the Czech Republic; in all the other countries with the exception of Russia the reporting levels for burglary decreased but not to any significant degree. Therefore, on average, the propensity to report burglary to the police has not changed in the period under observation. Reporting of robbery to the police increased significantly in the Czech Republic and Slovenia. It also increased somewhat in Russia and Poland, while it decreased in Estonia and Georgia. Only in Russia did the number of assaults reported to the police increase significantly; while it remained more or less at the same level in the other countries.

It would appear that the propensity to report to the police has not increased in most of the countries with the exception of the Czech Republic for both burglary and robbery, and Russia for all three types of crime considered here. It can be also noted that, on average, the propensity to report robberies has increased most.

Why do people report crimes to the police? The reasons are divided into: sense of civic duty ("should be reported"; "to stop it"); need for assistance ("to get help"); recovery/compensation of damage ("recovery of property"; "insurance"). "Want the offender caught/punished" lies somewhere between means for recovering property and damage and expectation for the law enforcement agency to effectively deal with offenders.

Civic duty related reasons are prominent across the board independently of crime type and developmental groupings. While this is true for "should be reported", reporting crime for preventive purposes "to stop it happening again" is of particular significance for threats/assaults or robbery while less so for burglary. This is quite a rational attitude on the part of the victims who also consider that reporting violent crimes has more chances of inducing preventive action by the police while burglary prevention is becoming much more the citizen's own prevention activity.

"To get help" as a reason for reporting is more frequently mentioned with relation to threats/assaults and robbery.

Recovery of property and insurance are both mentioned with respect to burglary and robbery. It is interesting to note that reporting for the reason of recovering property for both crimes is much more present among victims from countries in transition and the developing world than from the industrialised world. Inversely, insurance reasons are much more important in the industrialised world. There is a very clearly established pattern, according to which high insurance coverage results in high reporting rates in order to get the insurance premiums. Where insurance coverage is low, expectations related to reporting are to "recover" stolen property. Since the level of insurance coverage is much higher in the industrialised world than in countries in transition, the reasons for reporting in order to compensate for damage will reflect this discrepancy. "At the individual level, those without insurance are less likely to report burglaries to the police... At the aggregate level, there is always a strong association between the insurance coverage and reporting of burglaries to the police" (van Dijk, 1994). Indeed, the countries and regions with low insurance coverage tend to display low reporting rates of burglaries to the police.

Table 3. Reasons for reporting crime to the police, 1996

	Recover property	Insurance reasons	Should be reported	Want offender caught	To stop it	To get help	Other reasons
Burglary							
Western Europe	31.2	43.2	46.0	31.9	18.2	8.4	11.9
New World	17.4	22.8	51.1	27.2	13.0	8.7	15.2
Countries in transition	57.5	15.0	37.4	51.4	27.0	12.5	2.5
Asia	82.2	4.4	48.9	64.4	64.4	26.7	-
Africa	72.6	13.1	26.8	53.9	20.8	16.7	1.2
Latin America	53.2	26.2	19.5	42.9	34.8	8.6	3.1
Total	**52.4**	**20.8**	**38.3**	**45.3**	**29.7**	**13.6**	**6.8**
Robbery							
Western Europe	35.2	13.6	40.9	36.4	21.6	17.0	18.2
New World	23.3	13.3	56.7	46.7	26.7	20.0	16.7
Countries in transition	43.2	12.4	33.9	54.1	33.6	21.1	7.7
Asia	80.6	2.8	47.2	69.4	41.7	25.0	2.8
Africa	57.6	10.1	36.4	55.6	20.2	17.2	2.0
Latin America	39.0	32.0	23.0	54.0	40.5	17.0	3.0
Total	**46.5**	**14.0**	**39.7**	**52.7**	**30.7**	**19.6**	**8.4**
Assault/threat							
Western Europe	4.5	5.6	35.0	32.2	31.6	22.0	23.7
New World	6.9	6.9	36.2	39.7	39.7	24.1	22.4
Countries in transition	8.5	12.2	31.8	41.1	44.0	25.6	7.5
Asia	16.2	10.8	43.2	48.6	73.0	40.5	-
Africa	3.5	-	34.1	56.5	45.9	17.6	3.5
Latin America	18.0	42.4	18.7	38.8	44.6	22.3	7.2
Total	**9.6**	**15.6**	**33.2**	**42.8**	**46.5**	**25.4**	**12.9**

"Want the offender caught/punished" as a reason for reporting figures prominently for all three crimes. However, the differences in the importance of this particular reason between the regions are less pronounced when it comes to assault and robbery, and more pronounced when it comes to burglary. Most probably, the level of insurance coverage again is at play in a sense that for the victims of insured households to get the offender caught/punished is of less importance in terms of reporting to the police. On the other hand, if there is no household insurance, in order to recover property it is also important to find and punish the offender. In addition, there is a more punitive orientation in the developing countries and countries in transition (Zvekic, 1997) which also indicates the importance of this reason for reporting crime to the police.

It was noted that, on average, there are more non-reported crimes - in particular robberies and threats/assaults - in all the regions of the world and especially in countries in transition.

That the "police could do nothing" was frequently given as a reason for not reporting property crimes - thefts of personal property, thefts from cars, etc. This may signify a belief that the police would be unable to recover property, find the offender, or do anything else of benefit. It could also signify a fairly realistic judgement about the liability of the police to do much about something on which they have little information to act. In essence, though, it is an expression of resignation. In contrast, "the police wouldn't do anything" may carry a more explicit criticism that the police would be reluctant to take action, even though they might be expected to do so. "Fear/dislike of police" certainly signifies a negative attitude towards the police, either of a general nature, or related in some way to the particular offence in hand. As might be expected, fear and/or dislike of the police was often mentioned in relation to violent crimes and sexual incidents. These might involve a close relationship with the offender(s), or sometimes even a lifestyle that may lead the police to treat the victims as accomplices, or people "who deserve what they got". That women victims of sexual incidents are often treated unsympathetically by the police is also now well recognised.

Table 4 presents reasons for not reporting. Crimes are mainly not reported because they are not considered "serious enough". Since this section deals with the police, it is worth looking more clearly at police related reasons: "police could do nothing"; "police won't do anything" and "fear/dislike of police".

It should be noted that around 30% of the victims of burglary from the New World and even 52% from Asia thought that the burglary which took place in their household was "not serious enough"; this reason, together with "inappropriate for police", indicates the characteristics of the event itself. As regards robbery, "not serious enough" is mentioned as a reason for not reporting by 36%, 30% and 23% of the victims from Western Europe, Asia and countries in transition respectively. On the other hand, 22%, 26% and 15% of victims of assault/threats from Latin America, Africa and countries in transition mentioned the "inappropriateness" of the case for the police as reasons for non-reporting.

The resigned attitude towards the police ("police could do nothing") is particularly prominent among the victims of all three crimes dealt herewith from all but the industrialised world. As will be seen later, this has much to do with the expectations citizens have about the police as well as with satisfaction with the police in controlling and preventing crime.

The two more implicit criticisms of the police are also more pronounced reasons for not reporting the three crimes provided by victims from countries in transition. This is, however, more related to "police won't do anything". It should be noted that the implicit criticism that the police would be reluctant to take action is on average more highly related to robbery and assault/threats than to burglary.

"Fear/dislike" of police is mentioned significantly as a reason for not reporting robbery in Latin America and the New World as well as for assault/threats in Asia.

Table 4. Reasons for not reporting burglary, robbery and threats/assaults (1996)

	Not serious enough	Solved it myself	Inappropriate for the police	Other authorities	My family solved it	No insurance	Police could do nothing	Police won't do anything	Fear/dislike of police	Didn't dare	Other reasons	Don't know
Burglary												
Western Europe	26.2	21.4	4.8	-	7.1	4.8	16.7	2.4		2.4	21.4	8.1
New World	30.8	15.4	7.7	-	-	7.7	-	15.4	-	-	38.5	-
Countries in transition	27.0	13.3	13.2	6.6	9.0	6.5	28.4	16.7	5.6	6.8	8.6	9.4
Asia	52.4	13.3	14.3	2.9	3.8	2.9	14.3	5.7	11.5		3.8	3.8
Africa	17.4	12.3	10.7	7.1	5.5	2.4	35.2	12.3	2.8	6.3	14.2	4.3
Latin America	24.0	10.8	2.9	-	5.9	5.3	21.1	42.1	7.7	2.6	13.7	2.4
Total	29.6	14.4	8.9	5.5	6.3	4.9	23.1	15.8	6.9	4.5	16.7	5.6
Robbery												
Western Europe	35.7	10.7	17.9	1.8	5.4	-	25.0	7.1	5.4	7.1	16.1	2.7
New World	5.9	41.2	11.8	11.8	-	-	5.9		11.8	17.6	23.5	-
Countries in transition	23.4	12.7	10.3	1.7	6.4	8.0	30.9	27.7	13.5	9.9	9.7	6.5
Asia	30.4	10.1	18.8	4.3	10.1	1.4	30.4	17.4	9.1	10.1	4.3	-
Africa	14.7	9.6	10.9	-	1.9	0.6	46.8	14.7	5.1	12.2	16.7	1.9
Latin America	18.1	6.3	5.5	0.5	0.5	2.0	34.0	53.9	24.4	3.9	3.9	0.9
Total	21.4	15.1	12.5	4.0	4.9	3.0	28.8	24.2	11.6	10.1	12.4	3.0
Threat/ assault												
Western Europe	38.6	13.6	8.0	4.7	2.7	-	15.0	10.9	2.9	7.4	16.5	2.4
New World	25.6	17.9	7.7	6.4	2.6	-	6.4	15.4	5.1	5.1	28.2	5.1
Countries in transition	26.2	19.5	14.5	6.3	6.8	6.7	21.1	18.2	23.1	9.6	7.8	3.8
Asia	36.4	33.9	8.3	8.3	17.4	0.8	31.4	20.7	33.3	20.7	3.3	3.9
Africa	22.5	18.1	25.2	2.5	6.0	-	19.9	12.7	2.7	15.2	9.4	1.6
Latin America	17.4	30.7	21.8	0.7	4.2	1.6	14.9	26.1	6.9	9.6	6.2	1.8
Total	27.8	22.3	14.3	4.8	6.6	3.0	18.1	17.3	12.3	11.3	11.9	3.1

Satisfaction with the police

The ICVS also indicates the strength of police-community relations in showing: i) the degree of satisfaction victims feel when they report to the police; and ii) the reasons why victims were dissatisfied with the way the police handle cases once reported.

Table 5. Reasons for dissatisfaction with the police (1996)

	Did not do enough	Were not interested	Did not find offender	Did not recover goods	Gave no information	Incorrect/ impolite	Slow to arrive	Other reasons	Do not know
Burglary									
Western Europe	44.0	34.7	30.7	18.7	28.0	10.7	16.0	14.7	-
New World	75.0	25.0	25.0	20.0	25.0	10.0	20.0	20.0	-
Countries in transition	41.5	34.0	46.8	46.4	16.0	12.8	11.2	7.1	1.0
Asia	50.0	20.6	52.9	55.9	14.7	17.6	17.6	2.9	-
Africa	51.5	21.8	38.4	44.1	20.5	5.7	18.8	6.1	-
Latin America	55.8	41.4	34.5	32.1	26.1	20.9	4.8	3.6	0.8
Total	53.0	29.6	38.1	36.2	21.7	13.0	14.7	9.1	0.9
Robbery									
Western Europe	50.0	41.2	14.7	20.6	8.8	20.6	11.8	11.8	-
New World	40.0	40.0	40.0	6.7	13.3	20.0	13.3	6.7	-
Countries in transition	38.7	41.1	44.3	32.5	18.0	20.1	12.0	11.9	2.2
Asia	46.7	33.3	73.3	73.3	33.3	13.3	33.3	6.7	-
Africa	40.0	21.7	40 0	38.3	18.3	11.7	16.7	0.7	1.7
Latin America	56.0	53.6	44.0	26.4	29.6	18.4	9.6	0.8	-
Total	45.2	38.5	42.7	33.0	20.2	17.4	16.1	7.4	2.0
Assault/threat									
Western Europe	21.1	15.3	9.3	1.0	9.4	5.8	7.8	13.6	-
New World	23.4	14.3	10.0	-	14.3	-	10.0	12.2	-
Countries in transition	45.3	42.1	24.2	9.5	13.5	21.7	12.7	9.8	0.6
Asia	31.3	25.0	37.5	12.5	31.3	25.0	18.8	-	-
Africa	44.7	17.0	34.0	10.6	14.9	17.0	12.8	19.1	-
Latin America	50.0	44.9	34.6	6.4	25.6	29.5	11.5	2.6	-
Total	36.0	26.4	24.9	8.0	18.2	19.8	12.3	11.5	0.6

Among the reasons for dissatisfaction with the police once burglary was reported, the most frequently mentioned were "the

74

police did not do enough" and "were not interested". The first reason was identified by more than 40% of the burglary victims in countries in transition and up to 75% of those from the New World. Disinterest on the part of the police was mentioned by 41% of the victims in Latin America and one third of the victims in countries in transition and Western Europe.

A substantial portion (ranging from one third to more than a half) of the victims of burglary from the countries in transition also highlighted that the police "did not find the offender" or "did not recover goods". Indeed, in countries in transition, "want offender caught/punished" and "recovery of property" were among the principal reasons for reporting burglary to the police. Therefore, if these expectations are not met by the police, victims who reported burglaries express dissatisfaction highlighting unmet expectations. As mentioned earlier, in this part of the world, where insurance coverage is low, victims will have a substantial economic stake in reporting in order to retrieve stolen property or receive some compensation from the offender who needs to be identified and brought to justice.[2]

Victims of burglary from the developed world are more sensitive to other indicators of police performance such as providing appropriate information and speed or slowness of the police in arriving at the place of the crime.

Victims of robbery across the globe tend to emphasise that the police "did not do enough" (ranging from 40% in the New World and in countries in transition up to 56% in Latin America) and "were not interested" (from a peak of 54% in Latin America to 22% in Africa). More than 70% of the victims of robbery in Asia are dissatisfied with

---

2   For the preliminary analysis related to a restricted sample of countries in transition, see Zvekic (1996).

the police because the offender was not found and the goods were not recovered. Around 40% of the victims of robbery from Africa, Latin America and countries in transition express the same view. These two reasons for dissatisfaction are less prominent among the victims of robbery from Western Europe and the New World, although the latter give more importance to the offender being caught rather than to the goods being recovered.

The victims of assault/threats, particularly in countries in transition, single out that the reasons for dissatisfaction with the police reaction to reporting the crime have to do with the police not doing enough and not finding the offender. In addition, victims complain that the police were incorrect/impolite, which is more characteristic of the victims' evaluation of police attitudes in countries in transition. This factor indicates certain features of police culture that lacks respect for the particular needs and expectations of victims of violence.

Table 6. Satisfaction with police in controlling crime locally by regions (1996)

	Yes, good job	No, not a good job	Don't know
Total	45.8	38.8	16.8
Western Europe	54.0	25.6	20.4
New World	76.0	15.1	8.9
Countries in transition	23.2	40.0	36.7
Asia	58.3	30.7	11.0
Africa	41.1	51.7	7.2
Latin America	21.9	69.6	8.5

On the global level, less than half of the respondents are satisfied with the police in controlling crime locally, even though those who are satisfied are more than those who are not (Table 6). In the New World a large majority of the respondents (76%) are satisfied with the police in controlling crime; this is also the case with citizens from Western Europe (54%) and Asia (58%). On the other hand, more than half of the respondents from Africa (52%), 40% from countries in transition and as many as 70% from Latin America are not satisfied with the police job in controlling crime locally.

It should be noted that the lowest levels of citizens' satisfaction with the police are exhibited in Latin America and in countries in transition. However, it should also be noted that the largest percentage of "don't knows" is found in countries in transition. This can be explained by the fact that, during the period in which the 1992 ICVS was carried out, and - in some countries - also during the period when the 1996 ICVS was administered, the police were undergoing changes as to their mandates and organisation.

Table 7 shows that in the countries in transition that participated in both sweeps of the ICVS, the general level of satisfaction with the police controlling crime locally has, contrary to expectations, either decreased or remained at the same level. There were indeed some slight improvements in the citizens' evaluation in Estonia, Russia, and the Slovak and Czech Republics, but there was also a decrease in satisfaction both in Poland and Slovenia. As a matter of fact, what is really surprising is the still very high level of those that could not or refused to evaluate police performance in controlling crime locally. In both sweeps of the survey, with the exception of Slovenia in 1992, there was no country in transition in which the majority of the citizens were satisfied with the police, averaging some 23% of satisfied and some 40% of dissatisfied.

In 1992, apart from Slovenia, the highest level of satisfaction was expressed in Poland (one quarter). In 1996, again Slovenia was followed by Albania (the survey was carried out before the most recent Albanian crisis), Croatia, Macedonia (above 30%) and then

Romania, Mongolia, Bulgaria, Yugoslavia and the Slovak Republic (above 20%). However, it should be noted, that among these countries, more than half of the respondents in the Slovak Republic did not evaluate the police performance. This was the case in Albania, Bulgaria and Mongolia with some 40%, and in Croatia and Yugoslavia with some 30%. Around half of the respondents did not evaluate police performance in the Czech Republic, Latvia and Ukraine. In other countries the "don't knows" are also high (averaging 20%).

Table 7. Police do a good job: countries in transition, 1992-1996

	Good job		Not a good job		Don't know	
	1992	1996	1992	1996	1992	1996
Czech Republic	11.6	16.9	32.8	32.7	55.6	50.4
Estonia	9.4	15.9	54.3	46.1	36.3	38.0
Georgia	1.0	25.5	12.5	47.1	86.4	27.4
Poland	24.8	18.3	49.4	49.0	25.7	32.7
Russia	7.5	10.2	44.7	47.7	47.8	42.1
Slovak Republic	19.2	20.2	27.3	28.7	53.5	51.1
Slovenia	55.3	41.3	20.3	35.7	24.4	23.0
Albania	-	44.2	-	15.9	-	39.9
Belarus	-	19.1	-	33.5	-	47.3
Bulgaria	-	23.0	-	37.0	-	39.2
Croatia	-	37.9	-	29.5	-	32.6
Hungary	-	21.5	-	35.4	-	43.1
Kyrgyzstan	-	12.0	-	52.1	-	35.9
Latvia	-	14.6	-	36.0	-	49.3
Lithuania	-	14.1	-	65.7	-	20.2
Macedonia	-	34.7	-	39.0	-	26.3
Mongolia	-	24.7	-	36.4	-	39.0
Romania	-	28.1	-	53.0	-	18.9
Ukraine	-	15.6	-	37.7	-	46.3
Yugoslavia	-	25.5	-	42.7	-	31.7

Other factors related to police performance also have a lot to do with citizens' satisfaction. There is a moderate positive correlation between satisfaction with the police in controlling crime locally and frequency in local patrolling (0.349), although it is higher in both the developing world (0.382) and countries in transition (0.376) than in the industrialised world (0.165). In all likelihood, respondents in those parts of the world attach more importance to the presence of police locally in evaluating their performance in controlling crime locally. It might be the case that the citizens of the developing world and countries in transition consider that frequent police patrolling would deter crime and meet a number of their expectations such as finding and arresting offenders, recovering stolen goods and arriving speedily at the place of the crime. In addition, the citizens in countries in transition to a larger extent than citizens from the industrialised world are concerned that a burglary will occur within the next year. Therefore, fear of burglary in the near future also contributes to dissatisfaction with the police in controlling crime locally and supports the view that more frequent patrolling might be both deterrent as well as effective in "stopping crime", finding the offender and recovering the stolen property.

References

Findlay, M. and Zvekic, U. (1993). *Alternative Policing Styles: Cross-cultural Perspective*. Deventer, Boston: Kluwer.

Van Dijk, J.J.M. (1994). 'Who is afraid of the crime victim: criminal victimisation, fear of crime and opinions on crime in an international perspective'. Paper presented at the World Society of Victimology Symposium. Adelaide, Australia, 21-26 August 1994.

Zvekic, U. (1996). 'Policing and attitudes towards police in countries in transition'. In, Pagon, M. (Ed.), *Policing in Central and Eastern Europe, Proceedings of the International Conference*. Ljubljana, Slovenia, 14-16 November 1996.

Zvekic, U. (1997). 'Les attitudes des victimes envers la police et la punitivité: résultats des sondages internationaux de victimisation'. *Revue internationale de criminologie et de police technique*, Vol. I, Janvier-Mars.

CHAPTER 6

Appraisal of Security and Criminal Justice

People tend to appraise security and criminal justice on the basis of their own experience or by stories told, written or seen on TV. This appraisal is a mixture of rational and irrational elements, including fear for security and moral values as to what is just and what is not. This chapter discusses people's reactions to crime, victim support and punishment. In other words, reactions, expectations and values as related to different components of the crime process.[1]

Fear of crime is one of them. In this study it was measured by two indicators: feeling safe after dark and avoiding going out alone.

The respondents were asked how safe they feel when walking alone in their area after dark.

---

1   *Attitudes towards police were discussed in the previous chapter.*

Table 1. Street safety in world regions

	Very safe	Fairly safe	A bit unsafe	Very unsafe	Do not know
Western Europe	28.0	42.2	19.6	9.6	0.6
New world	26.9	40.7	18.5	13.5	0.4
Countries in transition	13.2	33.3	35.8	17.1	0.6
Asia	25.2	53.5	13.6	7.7	0.0
Africa	24.4	33.9	22.0	19.2	0.4
Latin America	18.9	32.5	26.6	21.7	0.3

These data reveal that street safety is perceived to be highest by citizens in Asia, followed by Western Europe and the New World. In Africa a bit less than 60% of the citizens feel safe. Just about a half of the citizens in Latin America feel very and fairly safe when walking alone after dark. The citizens that feel least safe are those in countries in transition, where 46% say they feel safe while 53% say they feel a bit unsafe or very unsafe. Among the world regions, the lowest percentage of citizens from countries in transition (13%) say they feel "very safe" in streets after dark.

Table 2. Street safety in countries in transition

	Very safe	Fairly safe	A bit unsafe	Very unsafe	Do not know
Estonia	9.5	29.6	44.7	16.2	
Poland	7.1	37.9	38.1	14.5	2.4
Czech Republic	9.6	32.3	39.7	18.5	
Slovak Republic	8.4	29.0	37.4	25.1	
Russia	9.5	22.0	43.9	24.6	
Georgia	30.8	27.9	34.1	7.2	
Slovenia	19.5	47.1	25.1	7.0	1.2
Latvia	6.3	25.1	41.2	26.9	0.5
Romania	9.3	38.8	27.7	23.8	0.3
Hungary	30.2	32.4	21.1	15.9	0.3
Yugoslavia	21.8	30.9	32.7	14.6	
Albania	11.0	44.3	32.4	8.1	4.2
Macedonia	32.4	31.6	28.8	6.4	0.7
Croatia	30.9	39.3	23.2	6.5	0.0
Ukraine	8.8	20.0	46.8	23.8	0.5
Belarus	6.8	30.5	41.7	20.0	1.0
Bulgaria	9.2	25.4	43.0	22.2	0.2
Lithuania	5.6	30.7	47.1	16.6	
Mongolia	13.0	53.4	26.0	7.5	
Kyrgyzstan	4.8	30.7	38.9	25.7	

Among the countries in transition, the highest levels of street safety are experienced by citizens from Croatia, Slovenia, Hungary, Macedonia and Mongolia. Those that feel the least safe are citizens from Ukraine, Russia and Latvia.

Table 3. Avoidance of places

	Yes	No	Do not know	Never go out
Estonia	41.0	48.8	2.6	7.6
Poland	48.1	41.0	1.9	9.0
Czech Republic	48.9	39.8	6.0	5.3
Slovak Republic	46.0	31.8	15.5	6.6
Russia	41.8	42.8	5.2	10.2
Georgia	19.1	68.6	6.7	5.5
Slovenia	37.8	52.3	5.9	4.1
Latvia	32.6	30.8	9.8	26.9
Romania	42.2	33.8	3.2	20.8
Hungary	36.6	46.2	3.2	14.0
Yugoslavia	49.7	39.1	5.0	6.2
Albania	38.8	49.7	5.9	5.6
Macedonia	28.9	66.2	3.7	1.2
Croatia	26.9	59.5	6.9	6.7
Ukraine	54.0	31.2	8.3	6.4
Belarus	45.3	33.5	8.8	12.4
Bulgaria	49.6	42.8	4.4	3.3
Lithuania	49.5	38.5	3.6	8.4
Mongolia	43.0	38.1	6.9	12.0
Kyrgyzstan	48.4	20.2	10.4	21.0

The respondents were also asked whether they avoid certain places after dark, and their response shows a high level of fear accompanied by proactive precautionary measures in Ukraine, Romania, Latvia and Kyrgyzstan (where more than 20% of the respondents said they never go out) as well as in Lithuania, Bulgaria, Yugoslavia and Poland.

These data reveal a diffused feeling of street unsafety among citizens in countries in transition. They also express a fear that they might be burglarised over the coming year.

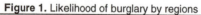
Figure 1. Likelihood of burglary by regions

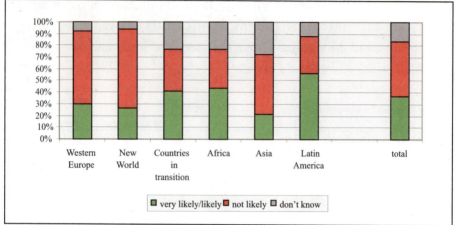

On a regional level, citizens in Latin America fear the most that they might be burglarised in the near future, followed by citizens in Africa and countries in transition; the citizens of the New World and Western Europe are less fearful.

Table 4. Likelihood of burglary in countries in transition

	Very Likely	Likely	Not very Likely	Unknown
Albania	2.30	38.30	42.50	16.90
Belarus	8.00	33.10	27.70	31.10
Bulgaria	25.60	41.30	20.20	13.00
Czech Rep.	6.20	35.00	34.80	23.90
Croatia	5.20	23.60	39.70	31.40
Estonia	4.10	23.70	41.20	31.00
Georgia	6.70	20.90	54.30	18.10
Hungary	3.20	25.20	45.50	26.10
Kyrgyzstan	5.00	44.90	34.70	15.50
Latvia	11.80	37.00	21.30	29.90
Lithuania	7.30	45.00	25.00	22.60
Macedonia	8.30	44.70	31.30	15.70
Mongolia	4.80	17.40	52.70	25.10
Poland	2.90	21.10	60.60	15.30
Romania	9.30	23.70	30.20	36.80
Russia	15.20	39.80	24.60	20.40
Slovak Republic	5.40	47.80	21.30	25.50
Slovenia	5.30	50.90	34.80	9.00
Ukraine	12.60	33.60	22.30	31.50
Yugoslavia	14.70	37.60	22.70	25.00

Among countries in transition, the citizens in Bulgaria, Russia, Slovenia, Yugoslavia, the Slovak Republic, Macedonia, Lithuania and Kyrgyzstan are the most fearful of being burglarised in the near future (over 50%). It should be noted that burglary as a very likely incident to take place in the near future is particularly felt by citizens in Bulgaria, Russia, Yugoslavia, Ukraine and Latvia. On the other hand, citizens in Poland, Georgia and Mongolia felt less threatened by the possibility of having their households burglarised in the near future.

Crime prevention measures

A pattern that is consistently observed in all the countries in transition is that of a low use of crime prevention measures despite a relatively high level of perceived likelihood of burglary and fear of crime.

Figure 2. Crime prevention measures by regions

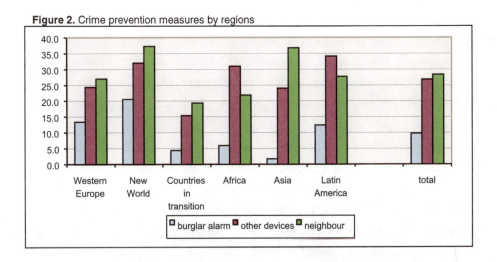

Table 5. Crime prevention measures in countries in transition

	Burglar alarm	Door locks	Special grills	Watch dog	High fence	Caretaker	Watch scheme	None	Ask neighbours
Albania	0.50	3.30	4.50	9.50	8.10	0.40	0.10	76.00	72.60
Belarus	5.70	12.70	1.10	9.50		4.50	17.00	55.20	30.60
Bulgaria	4.80	23.90	12.50	19.50	1.00	0.30	0.60	47.80	52.40
Czech Republic	4.60	49.80	4.40	26.50	5.80	2.30	18.90	22.90	26.00
Croatia	2.50	11.30	3.90	10.40	2.20	0.90	7.00	54.30	66.10
Estonia	2.80	17.20	2.60	23.80	1.60	0.30		58.60	32.70
Georgia	2.20	20.10	12.00	22.90	7.50	0.30	0.70	49.00	48.90
Hungary	7.40	52.00	18.70	29.80	7.90	1.20	2.00	15.60	68.60
Kyrgyzstan	2.70	24.60	19.50	22.70	6.40	0.20	1.80	40.50	58.90
Latvia	3.00	12.40	6.40	20.80	1.50	0.70	1.60	53.40	34.90
Lithuania	5.40	13.90	4.30	21.30	0.70	0.90	18.20	48.10	36.70
Macedonia	0.70	4.90	1.60	7.30	3.30		0.70	82.70	54.60
Mongolia	0.20	18.80	6.30	14.90	1.30	7.80	9.70	37.50	61.00
Poland	1.20	14.80	3.10	33.70	4.20	0.50	10.70	44.80	43.80
Romania	4.90	34.60	18.10	32.20	14.80			34.60	55.10
Russia	7.00	13.30	3.10	15.50		2.30	17.90	1.00	28.80
Slovak Republic	3.90	56.60	4.30	11.80	4.90	0.30	5.70	21.30	30.50
Slovenia	6.40	43.70	14.60	26.50	9.90	13.10	16.10		43.70
Ukraine	3.10	22.50	1.90	12.30	1.30	1.00	16.60	36.50	29.60
Yugoslavia	3.60	21.50	4.20	11.80	5.00	0.50	12.10	42.30	59.70

From a comparative perspective, it can be observed that different crime prevention measures are utilised in different regions of the world. On average, the most widespread measure used is some kind of neighbours' involvement in crime prevention, whether as part of a tradition or as part of designed and targeted programmes as it is the case mostly in the New World and Western Europe. Yet, even this measure is the least utilised in countries in transition. The same observation applies to burglar alarms, which are present in less than 5% of households in countries in transition as compared with 20% in the New World. Nor are other crime prevention devices and measures diffused in countries in transition.[2] In other words, countries in transition rank the lowest in terms of crime prevention measures. In

---

2   *Among other devices the most diffused are door locks and grills and the least diffused is the caretaker (with the exception of Slovenia).*

addition, insurance schemes are also not well developed or much utilised in countries in transition, thus leaving the citizens in a rather vulnerable position.

Table 6. Gun ownership rates and purpose of ownership, by regions (cities and urban areas)

	Western Europe	New World	Countries in transition	Asia	Africa	Latin America
Overall gun ownership rate	8.4	14.2	9.4	2.7	6.7	19.7
Rate of gun ownership for crime prevention purposes	0.8	1.7	2.9	1.4	3.7	14.3

Table 6 reveals that countries in transition rank third in the regional comparative perspective, both in terms of overall gun ownership rate as well as in terms of rate of gun ownership for crime prevention.

Table 7. Gun ownership rates and crime prevention purpose of ownership, by countries

Countries in transition	Ownership rate	Crime prevention purpose
Estonia	8.3%	50.5%
Poland	4.6%	44.0%
Czech Republic	21.2%	17.3%
Slovak Republic	3.3%	21.6%
Russia	9.2%	
Georgia	19.1%	26.7%
Slovenia	12.9%	7.9%
Latvia	10.5%	29.1%
Romania	2.3%	20.0%
Hungary	5.3%	25.0%
Yugoslavia	28.6%	35.1%
Albania	5.7%	1.5%
Macedonia	12.3%	15.1%
Croatia	14.4%	30.1%
Ukraine	5.9%	32.2%
Belarus	5.3%	15.1%
Bulgaria	11.4%	28.5%
Lithuania	7.1%	57.1%
Mongolia	6.6%	10.1%
Kyrgyzstan	9.9%	47.7%

Among countries in transition, the highest gun ownership rate is recorded in Yugoslavia and the Czech Republic but also in Georgia, Macedonia, Croatia, Slovenia and Bulgaria. It appears that countries that have experienced violent conflicts and civil wars such as Georgia and the former Yugoslavia exhibit the highest gun ownership rates.[3] As regards the crime prevention purpose of gun ownership, this is stated by more than a half of the Lithuanian and Estonian gun owners; close to 50% of the gun owners in Kyrgyzstan and Poland and from around a quarter to one third of gun owners from Hungary, Bulgaria, Croatia, Latvia, Georgia, Ukraine and Yugoslavia.

Victim assistance

Victims of crime who had reported to the police were asked whether they received support from a specialised victim support scheme. Furthermore, they were asked whether a specialised victim support agency would have been useful.

As expected, on average, only a few victims obtained any assistance, which was given mainly to victims of sexual offences and robbery in the New World and Western Europe. In the developed world, victims also expressed greater appreciation for the establishment of specialised victim support agencies. Such support is more evident in Latin America than in countries in transition and the rest of the developing world.

In countries in transition, on average less than 3% of the victims of burglary obtained some sort of assistance. More assistance

---

3   *It should be noted that these rates were recorded for capital cities and therefore it can be safely assumed that they are higher in rural areas. There is also a well-founded assumption that the rates recorded by the ICVS are lower than the real ones.*

was provided to victims of sexual offences and robbery. It is interesting to note that the greatest support for the establishment of such agencies is found among victims of robbery in Hungary, Albania, Ukraine, Russia and Poland and among victims of sexual offences. Particular support for the establishment of specialised victim assistance agencies is provided by victims of assault/threat in Hungary, Ukraine, Russia, the Czech Republic, Croatia and Macedonia.

Punishment orientation

Punishment is at the end of the criminal justice system. It can be seen as indicating societal reactions to crime; whether these are those of the state or people's notions of who, how and when should be punished. Yet, the range of sanctioning options in a given society is usually limited to a few that are selected by the legislator and a few which may fall outside the official sanctioning range (e.g. various forms of moral condemnation, or other forms of punishment which are neither recognised nor approved by the official penal code). Some of these alternatives may be harsher and some milder than those applied by the state-centred criminal justice system.

The ICVS asked respondents about sanctioning options, which are *usually* present in most criminal justice systems.[4] However, some options were not available in all the countries, and some that were available were not offered for comment. Another major limitation in measuring people's attitudes towards punishment stemmed from the

---

4   *The question was as follows: "People have different ideas about the sentences which should be given to offenders. Take for instance the case of a man 21 years old who is found guilty of a burglary for the second time. This time he stole a colour TV. Which of the following sentences do you consider the most appropriate for such a case: fine, prison, community service, suspended sentence or any other sentence?". If the interviewee opted for imprisonment, he/she was asked to specify the length.*

hypothetical burglary scenario used. It contained sufficient elements to help form a lay opinion, but lacked the most important details to provide for informed professional opinion.[5] Yet, it was felt that for the public at large, the particular details that may mitigate or aggravate the offender's position were unnecessary. There were, however, problems of interpretation linked with the target of theft: namely, a colour TV set, the value of which varies across countries. Indeed, as noted, the recovery of stolen goods is one driving factor in the evaluation of the police performance in less affluent economies. Nonetheless, certain patterns in punishment orientation emerged, in particular regarding differences between the more and less affluent societies.

Figure 3. Attitudes to punishment, imprisonment as preferred sanction by regions

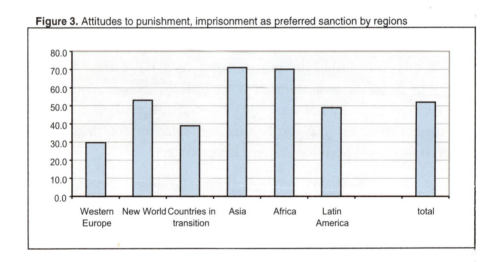

On a regional level, more than half of the respondents in the New World and Latin America and almost three-quarters in Asia and

---

5   There are serious doubts as to whether a professional judge would be able to state *what would be the most appropriate punishment based on the elements provided by the ICVS questionnaire.*

Africa opted for imprisonment. On the other hand, some 40% of the respondents from countries in transition and somewhat less than a third from Western Europe favoured imprisonment.

Following imprisonment, the next most preferred sentencing option was community service, which was favoured by almost one third of the respondents. In Western Europe, community service was the preferred sentence by almost half of the respondents, followed by approximately one third each in Latin America and in countries in transition. Only 10% of the respondents from Asia and Africa opted for some sort of community service.

Regional variations regarding a fine as a favoured sentencing option for a young recidivist burglar are not pronounced and average 9% of the respondents. A suspended sentence is thought to be the most appropriate sentence by 5% of the respondents; ranging however from 2% in Asia and Africa respectively to 7% in the countries in transition and Western Europe.

Table 8. Attitudes to punishment, preferred sanction, countries in transition

	Fine	Prison	Community service	Suspended Sentence	Other Sentence	Unknown
Albania	20.40	62.90	7.20	3.00	3.50	3.00
Belarus	15.60	40.20	28.90	1.50	3.10	10.80
Bulgaria	3.50	39.80	45.30	5.50	3.70	2.20
Czech Republic	5.10	35.10	38.60	12.00	3.00	6.10
Croatia	7.10	14.80	67.60	5.80	1.80	2.90
Estonia	3.50	44.30	32.30	8.40	6.00	5.50
Georgia	26.70	33.70	21.30	13.50	0.80	4.00
Hungary	11.40	32.70	41.10	4.80	5.40	4.50
Kyrgyzstan	13.70	25.50	35.50	22.80	2.10	0.40
Latvia	11.70	48.00	20.30	11.30	5.40	3.40
Lithuania	15.40	41.00	30.10	4.40	5.30	3.80
Macedonia	11.50	40.70	24.50	11.90	2.90	8.50
Mongolia	8.60	41.40	2.00	2.00	12.30	33.80
Poland	6.40	18.00	62.80	6.30	3.40	3.10
Romania	1.30	59.40	25.80	1.30	7.80	4.50
Russia	6.40	48.80	26.90	2.60	7.10	8.20
Slovak Republic	4.80	36.30	42.90	6.90	4.70	4.40
Slovenia	9.90	35.80	41.30	6.00	2.10	4.90
Ukraine	14.40	38.20	33.30	1.50	1.50	6.80
Yugoslavia	5.60	42.30	38.40	6.40	2.70	4.60

Among the countries in transition, the most preferred sanction is imprisonment, particularly in Albania, Romania, Russia, Latvia, Estonia and Yugoslavia. After imprisonment, the second most preferred sentence is community service, especially in Croatia, Poland, Bulgaria, Hungary, Slovenia, and the Slovak and Czech Republics.

Both the 1992 (Kuhn, 1993) and 1996 ICVS (Zvekic, 1997) support Kuhn's finding that those who had been victimised were no more in favour of a prison sentence than others, both at the global and regional levels. There is no significant difference in preferences for sentencing options between victims and non-victims of any crime. A group of special interest as regards the punishment of the burglar is that of those who had been burgled themselves. However, there is no substantial difference between the victims and non-victims of burglary, with the exception of burglary victims from the New World who appear to be stronger supporters of imprisonment than non-burglary victims, still within the prevailing prison-centric orientation in that part of the world. Further analyses carried out on victims and non-victims of contact crimes and vehicle-related crimes also confirmed the above-mentioned finding.

The demand for severe punishment, then, is stronger in the more crime-ridden nations or in those in which there is a lack of alternative solutions including an adequate insurance coverage. There, ideas about preventive approaches to sentencing may appear less appropriate. Deterrent sentencing, regardless of whether or not it is effective, may have more appeal.

There is a certain level of correspondence in the regional patterns based on public attitudes to punishment, on the one hand, and the predominant actual use of non-custodial sanctions and imprisonment, on the other. This seems to indicate at least two things: first, a degree of independence in types of sentencing from the geo-political and development position; second, that public attitudes do reflect, to a certain degree, the actual availability of sentencing options and their use in practice. In other words, public attitudes are influenced by penal systems and penal practice, although neither exclusively nor in a clearly pre-deterministic manner (Zvekic, 1997b).

In countries in transition much work is still needed to promote credible non-custodial sanctions and in particular to overcome difficulties in implementation following conviction. In fact, public attitudes often lag behind sentencing reform and time is needed to convey the message that punishment is implemented seriously in order to ensure public acceptance. Support for imprisonment is often formed by vicarious information, traditional belief systems and socio-legal heritage. Fear of crime also appears to support harsher sentencing. All of this is not an irrational response to urgent crime problems. Where the replacement of stolen property is relatively easy, either through insurance coverage or through the ability to buy new commodities, severe punishment is not the obvious cure. However, where - as is the case in the majority of countries in transition - hardship precludes replacing stolen property, calls for more severe punishment, bringing offenders to justice and the recovery of stolen goods are rational responses to crime problems.

References

Kuhn, A. (1993). 'Attitudes towards punishment'. In, Alvazzi del Frate, A., Zvekic, U. and van Dijk, J.J.M. (Eds.), *Understanding Crime: Experiences of Crime and Crime Control*. Rome: UNICRI

Zvekic, U. (1997). 'Les attitudes des victimes envers la police et la punitivité: résultats des sondages internationaux de victimisation', *Revue internationale de criminologie et de police technique*, Vol. I, Janvier-Mars.

Zvekic, U. (1997b). 'International trends in non-custodial sanctions'. In, Villé, R, Zvekic, U. and Klaus, J., *Promoting Probation Internationally*. Rome: UNICRI.

CHAPTER 7

Summary and Discussion

The main aims of the ICVS in general and as regards countries in transition in particular were to: provide comparative indicators of crime and victimisation risks, performance of law enforcement, victim assistance and crime prevention; promote crime surveys as an important research and policy tool at the international, national and local levels; enhance adequate research and policy analysis methodology; create an opportunity for transparency in public debate about crime and reactions to crime; strengthen public and criminal justice concerns about citizens' participation in the evaluation of criminal policy and particularly in partnership in crime prevention; and finally, promote international co-operation by providing an opportunity for a large number of countries to share methodology and experience through their participation in a well co-ordinated international research project.

The twenty countries in transition that took part in the ICVS both gained from this experience and significantly contributed to it. Although the ICVS is of an international comparative nature, it is also very much a national endeavour. One of its most important aims was to promote both regular participation in future sweeps of the ICVS as well as the carrying out of self-sustained and targeted national and local surveys. This is of particular importance for countries in transition since for most of them the ICVS was their first experience with such surveys. Moreover, in the majority of them, the ICVS was carried out only in the largest city and therefore there is a need to expand it on a national level, on the one hand, and to focus it on local situations, on the other. The three suggested developments (international, national and local) go hand in hand.

As noted in Chapter 1, countries in transition represent a very heterogeneous group of countries according to level of development, culture, geopolitical position and the depth and magnitude of changes following the downfall of the communist system. However, the term "countries in transition" stands in essence for post-communist societies and this is their main common characteristic. This common political experience should not be undermined but neither should it be given too much emphasis. Yet, while each of them - particularly those that gained independence following the dismantling of USSR, Czechoslovakia and Yugoslavia - attempts to pursue its own path of development, this is becoming limited in view of at least four interrelated processes. First, the common political and cultural heritage itself sets limits to the ways and modes of social, political and economic change. Second, the prevailing model of a market economy and political arrangements as experienced by the West also limit options since they set the aims and - more often than not - the means to achieve them. Third, economic and political regional integration as well as the world-wide process of globalisation streamlines economic and political developments in countries in transition. Finally, international assistance in the process of reform sets certain methods and standards that are requested or expected to be followed and met. This is all to say that, to a large extent, countries in transition, despite many differences, share a similar economic and political heritage and pretty much similar economic and political developments in the future.

Crime appears to be one of the features that countries in transition have in common as a group and as members of the new economic and political set-up. They definitely share an increase in many forms of conventional crime for which both the official criminal justice statistics as well as the ICVS provide ample evidence. They also share common experiences with corruption for which the ICVS again provides evidence, and with transnational and local organised crime. Countries in transition, in addition to the above, still share in common a rather negative perception of law enforcement activities on the part of citizens, lack of victim assistance and a lack of developed and effective crime prevention. Citizens in countries in transition feel rather insecure because of crime threats; many promptly state that this feeling of insecurity increased in the period of transition as compared with the previous period. In this respect, and coupled with the financial strains under which many people in countries in transition still live, there is a rather diffused punitative attitude even for non-violent crimes such as burglary.

This is not to say that all countries in transition have the same levels of crime and insecurity. Indeed, even the crime types differ within the group. As the analysis of country profiles of crime and trends in crime revealed (only for six countries which took part both in the 1992-94 and 1996-97 sweeps):

- burglary participates in crime totals more substantially in countries in transition than in industrialised countries, accounting for some 20% of crime totals in almost one third of the countries in transition; it increased in three countries and also decreased in three countries;
- somewhere between 20% and a quarter of crime totals are composed of violent personal crime (robbery, assaults/threats and sexual offences) in almost three quarters of the countries in transition; there was an increase in four countries (a rather substantial increase in two of them) as regards assault, as well as an increase in robbery in five countries in transition;
- theft of and from car make up one third of crime totals in almost one third of the countries in transition, and somewhere between 20% and a quarter of crime totals in a further nine countries in transition; car theft increased in four and decreased in two countries in transition;
- theft of personal property is much diffused (over 20% of crime totals) in just over half of the countries in transition with peaks of 42% and a minimum of 12%; it increased in all the six countries that took part in both the second and the third sweeps of the ICVS;
- consumer fraud in countries in transition shows the highest rate in the regional comparative perspective with country rates over 50% in one third of the countries in transition; and
- corruption is one of the most diffused forms of victimisation in countries in transition.

The ICVS in countries in transition, but also in other countries, highlighted the needs of crime victims. Many respondents pointed out concerns to stop what happened to them and called for help. Most of them were not satisfied either with the police response or with that received from some other agencies or mechanisms. Many of the respondents, and particular victims of violent crimes, expressed strong support for the establishment of specialised victim assistance schemes and/or agencies.

Similarly, the results of the ICVS point out great problems with crime prevention measures in countries in transition. Neither informal schemes, such as neighbourhood watch, nor crime prevention devices are readily available to most citizens in countries in transition. Obviously, without self-precautionary measures and without adequate economic and social incentives to facilitate the introduction of crime prevention initiatives and devices, there will be more crime with higher and unequally distributed costs. All of these will also have consequences in furthering social stratification, including unequal crime risks, as well as in increasing citizens' expectations towards law enforcement and criminal justice, and thus reducing the level of confidence in the public authority structure.

The above observation leads to a consideration of two related issues which merit special attention in countries in transition: corruption in public administration, and the relationship between citizens and the police. Each of them indicates certain concerns with the process of reform of society and in particular that of the criminal justice system.

Corruption in public administration

Although the level of bribery by public officials varies greatly by regions and countries, the ICVS findings indicate that public officials' involvement in, and exposure to, bribery merit special attention in countries in transition in terms of developing an adequate anti-corruption consciousness and effective regulatory, control and grievance/appeals mechanisms within the public administration. These would contribute towards the reduction of corruption as well as towards increasing citizens' confidence in the public administration's willingness and capacity to effectively deal with corruption cases involving public officials. Much of street level corruption is a problem of public administration organisation and culture. It appears that - particularly in a number of countries in transition - further efforts are needed in order to improve the social status of, and compensation for, public officials, thus making them less "vulnerable" to the challenges of bribery. Reforms are also needed in terms of facilitating and making more transparent both the decision-making process as well as interaction with citizens. Corruption in public administration appears to be particularly diffused where public administration is still much more an exercise in power over the citizens rather than a service to citizens. In a number of societies things are further complicated by certain cultural patterns that favour corrupt relations and "justify" corrupt transactions. Corruption in public administration is very much a problem of democracy, organisation of public administration and political culture as it is very much a problem of economic stability and a market culture. Corruption in public administration is a particularly difficult problem to deal with in those societies in which there is a *tout court* low level of confidence between the citizenry and public administration as well as in those in which discretionary power to decide over public and/or private affairs is very much concentrated within the political regime or the financial-political centres of power. As a rule, corruption goes hand in hand with the abuse of power, political and economic monopoly and organised crime. Therefore, the cultural, political, economic and legal means - including criminal justice - to prevent and fight corruption cannot be divorced from broader processes of political democratisation, economic and social

100

development and certainty of financial and legal transactions. As noted, corruption in administration stands for a visible test of the changes achieved with respect to democratisation, rule of law and citizens' status in countries in transition.

From an UNICRI study on corruption in nineteen countries in transition[1] the following problems were identified particularly related to the role of criminal justice in the fight against corruption.

On the side of prevention the measures suggested may include:

- increase fair competition;
- reduce monopolies in the market;
- enact an adequate economic and social policy;
- introduce checks and balances for decision makers;
- increase transparency in public administration and simplify administrative procedures;
- introduce integrity testing, auditing procedures and structures;
- enhance legislation and control of corruption vulnerable sectors;
- improve controls over banks, including removal of bank secrecy, encouragement of detecting and reporting of corruption, and reduction of cash transactions; and
- provide more information to public and raise public awareness.

---

1   In April 1997 and May 1998, UNICRI organised the First and Second Seminars on Anti-corruption Strategies for Central and Eastern European Countries held at the International Law Enforcement Academy (Budapest, Hungary) in which international experts and representatives from police and public prosecution of 9 and 10 countries in transition respectively took part. The results of the analysis based on information prepared for and discussed during the Seminars are presented in: Hiroyuki Shinkai (Ed.) 'Combating Corruption in Central and Eastern Europe'. UNICRI series Issues & Reports, No.10/1997 and the Report of the Second Seminar, UNICRI, July 1998 (unpublished).

In the area of legislation the following obstacles were identified:

- lack of comprehensive anti-corruption laws including lack of provisions to extend corruption to the private sector and foreign officials;
- lack of clear provisions regarding certain investigative techniques such as:
- wiretapping and/or electronic surveillance; undercover agents; witness protection and means of securing their testimony; inaccessibility to investigate private banks and international transactions; and
- lack of the concept of corporate liability.

Among the organisational, skill-related and information related obstacles were:

- lack of co-operation among national agencies, with other countries and with international organisations;
- no provisions for inter-organisational co-operation;
- lack of financial resources and technical equipment to carry out special investigation techniques;
- lack of a good database and network to ensure the analysis and monitoring of corruption trends and cases as well as of an information exchange among different agencies dealing with corruption;
- the low social status of criminal justice personnel;
- difficulty in recruiting competent personnel; and
- lack of intra-organisational auditing, monitoring and/or problems in implementing codes of conduct.

Strategies to fight corruption do not reside only with criminal justice but rather they belong to the economic and social policy arena and the development of a civic political culture. Corruption is a process and a relationship, and therefore the state, its public administration and the citizens all share responsibility in preventing and controlling it, although not to the same extent.

Citizens and police: confidence building in the process of democratisation

The lowest levels of citizens' satisfaction with the police are exhibited in countries in transition and Latin America. Indeed, in both sweeps of the ICVS with the exception of Slovenia in 1992, there was no country in transition in which the majority of citizens were satisfied with the police, averaging some 23% of satisfied and some 40% of dissatisfied citizens. Furthermore, reporting to the police of cases of robbery and assault is among the lowest in the comparative perspective although this is not the case for burglaries; the propensity to report to the police has not increased in most countries in transition. Thus, one of the most powerful indicators of changes in terms of confidence building between citizens and the police in countries in transition does not provide a satisfactory picture.

The evaluation of police performance seems to be a rational process within a given context. Victims' expectations of interested and efficient treatment from the police in the developed world reflect a concern with citizens' rights, good service delivery by the police, and reliance on insurance mechanisms for damage recovery. The recovery of stolen property and bringing offenders to justice is the rational response of victims in less affluent, less "insured" and more crime-ridden societies. There is no doubt that satisfaction with the police is higher in the developed world and in the more affluent regions. Here, other public services are also probably more accessible and of a better quality.

In terms of crime prevention and control, the ICVS confirms that public safety is still very much police business, and that citizens in countries in transition expect more police presence and more police efficiency, as a minimum. Seeking safety, less crime and less fear of crime is a process in which all parties have a role to play.

There appears to be a strong relationship between satisfaction with police performance, crime reporting and frequency of patrolling. These findings strongly support the idea that an elementary requirement for good policing in crime prevention consists in a systematic police presence, which increases both the feeling of safety among citizens and satisfaction with the police. Needless to say, these are both in turn important for public security. An increased feeling of safety that has to do with police presence increases public satisfaction with and confidence in the police. This is not a matter of more investment in the number of personnel and/or equipment, or rather not only that. It is much more a matter of a more rational policy for the allocation of resources, and it is very much a matter of a general democratisation of public institutions and services to be made sensitive to the needs of the clients and accountable to the public. It is also a matter of changes in the culture of the police-citizen relationship. Such a change requires, at the same time, both more and less than what conventional skill-related training, better equipment and other types of assistance are able to provide for.

There is still a lot of dissatisfaction with the police, particularly in terms of the ways in which they deal with reported cases and control residential areas. The fear that a burglary will occur in the near future is widely diffused. Despite investments in police reform, the overall results as evaluated by citizens and victims are far from satisfactory. Citizens are concerned with outcomes, everyday police behaviour and the police culture in general. All these take place in a wider context of the socio-economic and political changes and the development of service orientation and practice of public administration, including the police.

The police should concentrate on improving outcomes of the organisation: lowering the victimisation rate, improving the perceived safety and the level of safety problems experienced by the population, preventing public order problems and improving confidence in the police. Reaching these objectives is a rational measure of police performance and evaluation. The citizens' evaluation of the police is a rational reflection of crime concerns and police behaviour in servicing the community. For crime prevention and control and for justice in society it is at least no less important than any other device developed for the internal measurement of police success. There is still much to be desired in changing the police culture and improving police-community relations in countries in transition.

The ICVS is an important research and policy/management tool for screening and evaluating the present and for identifying directions for future work. Hence, this call for countries in transition to develop their own surveys and promote public debate on crime concerns as well as to join the next ICVS sweep.

ЖЕРТВЫ ПРЕСТУПНОСТИ В СТРАНАХ В ПЕРЕХОДНОЙ СТАДИИ

Конспект и Обсуждение

Основными целями Международного Исследования Жертв Преступлений (МИЖП), как в основных, так и в относящихся к ним странах, находящихся в переходной стадии, в частности, было: обеспечивать сравнительными показателями преступлений и преследований, подвергшихся риску; приведение в исполнение законов, помощь пострадавшим и предупреждение преступлений; содействовать исследованию преступлений, как важного изучения и инструмента политики на международном, национальном и местном уровнях; увеличивать отвечающие требованиям исследования и политический анализ методологии; создание возможной гласности общественных дебатов преступлений и реакции выноса приговора; укреплять общественное и уголовное правосудие, касающиеся гражданских лиц, принимающих участие в оценке уголовной политики и, особенно, в сотрудничестве по предупреждению преступлений; и, наконец, способствовать международному содействию в обеспечении как можно большего числа стран делить методологию и опыт посредством их участия в продуманно скоординированном международном исследовании проекта.

Двадцать стран, находящиеся в переходной стадии приняли участие в МИЖП, внеся приобретённый опыт и сделав значительный вклад. Несмотря на то, что МИЖП, является по сути сравнительно международным, он также представляет очень большую национальную попытку. Одной из наиболее важных целей было поддержать как регулярное участия в будущих действиях МИЖП, так и завершить до конца как самоподдерживающие, так и объекты национального и местного исследования. Это особенно важно для стран в переходной стадии с тех пор, как для многих из них МИЖП стал их первый опыт с подобным исследованием. Более того, для большинства стран, МИЖП выполнялся только в крупных городах, поэтому и существует необходимость расширять его на национальном уровне, с одной стороны, и фокусировать на местных ситуациях, с другой. Три предложенных развития (международное, национальное и местное) идут рука в руку.

Страны в переходной стадии представляют очень неоднородную группу государств, согласно уровню развития культуры, геополитическому положению и глубине и значимости изменений, ведущих к разрушению коммунистической системы. Однако, термин "страны в переходной стадии" применяется, в сущности, для пост-коммунистического общества и это одна из основных их характеристик. Такой общий политический опыт не должен учитываться и не стоит его подчёркивать. До сих пор, пока все они - особенно те, которые приобрели независимость вслед за развалом СССР, Чехословакия и Югославия - пытаются следовать своим собственным путём развития, это становится ограниченным с точки зрения, по крайней мере, четырёх взаимосвязанных процессов. Первый, общее политическое и культурное наследие, которое само по себе лимитирует пути и методы социальных, политических и экономических изменений. Второй, превалирующая модель рынка экономической и политической договорённости как показывает опыт Запада, также ограничивается выбор, с того момента как они наметили цели и - более чаще чем нет - средств достигнуть их. Третий, экономическое и политическое региональное интегрирование как широкий мировой процесс глобального устремления экономического и политического развития стран в стадии перехода. Наконец, международная помощь в процессе реформ, стабилирует методы и стандарты, которые должны или могут быть применяться или признаваться. Всё это говорит о том, что для большинства стран, находящихся в переходной стадии, несмотря на многим различиям есть доля схожести экономического и политического наследия и очень похожего экономического и политического развития в будущем.

Преступность возникает как одна из характеристик стран в переходной стадии имеющих общую как группу, так и членов новой экономической и политической системы. Они определённо разделяют увеличение во многих формах обычную преступность о которой, как официальная статистика уголовного правосудия, так и МИЖП снабжает достаточными фактами. Они также делят общий опыт с коррупцией, о котором МИЖП, опять же предоставляет факты, как и о транснациональной и местной организованной преступности. Страны в переходной стадии, в добавлении к вышесказанному, ещё делят, в общем, и негативное восприятие закона об усилении деятельности со стороны граждан, о недостатке помощи жертвам и о недостатке развития эффективного предотвращения преступности. Граждане стран в переходной стадии чувствуют ощутимую незащищённость из-за угрозы преступлений; многие заявляют без сомнения, что данное чувство беззащитности увеличилось в период стадии перехода по сравнению с предыдущим периодом. В данном отношении и связанность с финансовыми злоупотреблениями, в условиях которых ещё многие люди в странах в переходной стадии продолжают жить, это довольно-таки распространена тенденция к наказанию, даже для таких не опасных преступлений, как кража.

Это не говорит о том, что все страны в переходной стадии имеют одинаковый уровень преступности и незащищённости. Конечно, даже виды преступности отличаются от групп. Анализ краткого очерка преступности и тенденций преступности в стране показывает (только в шести странах, которые принимали участие в действиях, как в 1992-94 и так и в 1996-97):

- кража с нападениями составляет большой процент общего количества преступлений в странах в переходной стадии, чем промышленных, так как приблизительно 20% одной трети из стран в переходной стадии; она увеличилась в трёх странах и также в трёх странах сократилась;
- приблизительно между 20% и четверти преступлений всего составляют виды одиночных преступных нападений (грабёж, угрожающее словесное оскорбление/угроза и сексуальные нападения) почти в трети четверти стран в стадии перехода; произошло увеличение в четырёх странах (особо существенно увеличилось в двух из них), как нападения с угрозой, так и грабёжи увеличились в пяти странах находящихся в переходной стадии;

- воровство и кражи машин составляют одну треть преступлений в почти в одной трети стран в переходной стадии, и где-то между 20% и четверть преступлений насчитывается в других девяти странах в переходной стадии; угон машин увеличился в четырёх и сократился в двух странах в переходной стадии;

- кража частной собственности очень распространилась (более чем на 20% преступлений в целом) только около половины стран в стадии переходного периода, где пик достиг 42% и минимум 12%; увеличение произошло во всех шести странах, принимающих участие как во втором, так и в третьем действии МИЖП;

- процент потребительского мошенничества в странах в переходной стадии максимальный в региональной панораме, и в одной трети стран в переходной стадии процент свыше 50%; и

- коррупция - самая распространённая форма обмана в странах, находящихся в переходной стадии.

МИЖП в странах переходной стадии, но также и в других странах, выдвинулась на первый план необходимость преступлений жетрв. Многие выступающие подчеркивали в этой связи прекратить то, что произошло с ними и взывали о помощи. Многие не были удовлетворены откликами полиции или тем, что они получили от некоторых агенств или государственных аппаратов. Многие выступающие, и особенно жертвы криминальных преступлений, высказывают сильную поддержку в создании агенств и/или программ специальной помощи жертвам.

Аналогично, результами МИЖП подчеркнул важную проблему о мерах предотвращения преступности в странах, находящихся переходной стадии. Ни негосударственные программы, такие как контролирование кварталов, ни не инструменты для предотвращения преступности легко доступны для большей части граждан стран в переходной стадии. Очевидно, что без мер самопредосторожности и без соответствующих экономических и социальных стимулов чтобы способствовать введению инициатив и планов для предотвращения преступности, возникнет ещё больше преступности с высокой и неравной распределительной ценой. Всё это и будет иметь дальнейшие последствия социальной стратификации, включая несправедливый риск преступлений, как увеличение ожидания граждан дальнейшего усиления закона и криминального правосудия, и тем самым сокращение уровня доверия в официальным структурам органов власти.

Из вышеупомянутого обзора следует, то что необходимо принять во внимание два взаимосвязанных издания, которые заслуживают особого внимания в странах в переходной стадии: коррупция в государственном управлении, и взаимоотношения граждан и полиции. Каждый из них указывает на заботу согласно процесса реформы общества и особенно системы криминального правосудия.

Коррупция в государственном управлении

Даже если уровень взяточничества должностными лицами в большой степени зависит от региона и страны, полученные МИЖП данные указывают на то, что привлечение и разоблачение официальных лиц во взяточничестве заслуживает специального внимания в странах находящихся в переходной стадии в сроке развития адекватного анти-коррупционного осознания и эффективного регулярного контроля и недовольство/жалоб механизмов государственного управления. Это может внести вклад как на дальнейшее сокращение коррупции, так и на дальнейшее увеличение доверия граждан в государственном управлении готовности и способности эффективно занимающихся делами коррупции, в которые привлечены должностные лица. Многие обычные виды коррупции это проблема организации государственного управления и культуры. Она появляется - особенно в ряде стран находящихся в переходной стадии - как дальнейшие силы нуждающиеся для того чтобы улучшить социальный статус и зарплаты должностных лиц, делая их менее "уязвимыми" к возражению против взятки. Реформы также необходимы в сроки облегчения и создания большей гласности, как при принятии решения процесса, так и для взаимоотношений с гражданами. Коррупция в государственном управлении как бы особо распространилась там, где государственное управление всё ещё имеет значительную власть над гражданами, при этом не для службы граждан. В ряде обществ дела обстоят гораздо сложнее, из-за некоторых культурных образцов, которые благоприятствуют отношениям к взятке и "оправдывают" взятку в комерческих операциях. Коррупция в государственном управлении - это большая проблема демократии, организации государственного управления и политической культуры, с тех пор, как эта проблема экономической стабильности и культуры рынка. Коррупция в государственном управлении - это особенно сложная проблема, касающаяся того общества, в котором очень низкий уровень доверительности между гражданскими лицами и государственным управлением, также как в тех, где дискреционная власть решать над долностными и/или частными делами очень сосредоточена с политическим режимом или финансово-политическим центром власти. Как правило, коррупция идёт рука в руку со злоупотреблениями власти, политической и экономической монополией и организованной преступностью. Поэтому, культурные, политические, экономические и легальные инструменты - включая уголовное правосудие - для предотвращения и борьбы коррупции не могут быть отделены от широких процессов политической демократизации, экономического и социального развития и, безусловно, финансовых и легальных коммерческих операций. Как уже замечено, коррупция в управлении это реальное измерение изменений, достигнутых в отношении демократизации, правил законов и условий граждан в странах в переходной стадии.

Исходя из изучений ЮНИКРИ о коррупции в девятнадцати странах, находящихся в стадии перехода [1], следующие проблемы были идентифицированы, особенно связанные с ролью криминального правосудия в борьбе против коррупции.

Со стороны предотвращения предлагаемые меры могут включать:

- увеличение справедливого соперничества;
- сокращение монополий на рынке;
- принятие адекватной социальной и экономической политики;

---

1   В Апреле 1997 и в Мае 1998, ЮНИКРИ организовал Первый и Второй семинар по Анти-коррупции и Стратегии в Странах Центральной и Восточной Европы, состоявшийся в Международной Академии по праву применения (Будапешт, Венгрия), где международные специалисты и представители из полиции и государственной прокуратуры из 9 и 10 стран находящихся в переходной стадии, соответственно, приняли участие. Результаты анализов базирующихся на информации подготовленной и обсуждённой во время Семинаров были представлены: Хироюки Шинкай (Изд.) "Борьба с Коррупцией в Центральной и Восточной Европе". ЮНИКРИ серия *Издание и Доклады*, 10/1997 и Доклад Второго Семинара, ЮНИКРИ, Июль 1998 (не опубликован).

- введение проверки и баланса для тех кто решает;
- увеличение гласности в государственном управлении и упрощение административных процедур;
- введение тестов неподкупности, процедур и инструментов контроля;
- увеличение законодательств и контроля коррупции в уязвимых секторах;
- улучшение контроля за банками, включая передачи банковских секретов, ободрение при обнаружении и контролировании коррупции, и сокращение коммерческих операций за наличный расчёт; и
- обеспечение большей информацией масс и повышение общественной ответственности.

В области законодательства, следующие препятствия были найдены:

- недостаток окончательных анти-коррупционных законов, включающих расширенные положения о законе коррупции в частном секторе и зарубежными официальными лицами;
- недостаток чётких положений относительно некоторых техник исследования таких как:
- прослушивание и/или электронное наблюдение; переодетые агенты; защита свидетелей и средства безопасности их показаний; недоступность расследования частных банков и международных коммерческих операций; и
- отсутствие понятия о корпоративной принадлежности.

Среди организационной, квалифицированной и информации связанной с препятствиями были:

- отсутствие сотрудничества среди национальных агенств, с другими странами и с международными организациями;

- не обеспеченность внутриорганизационного сотрудничества;
- отсутствие финансовых ресурсов и технического оборудования для завершения специальной техники исследования;
- отсутствие хорошей базы и сети гарантирования анализов и прослушивание общих тенденций и случаев как информационного обмена среди различных агенств, занимающихся коррупцией;
- низкий социальный статус персонала уголовного правосудия;
- трудности в комплектовании компетентного персонала; и
- отсутствие внутриоганизационных ревизий, контроля и/или проблемы в осуществлении норм поведения.

Стратегии по борьбе с коррупцией не свойственны только криминальному правосудию, но принадлежат экономической и социальной политике и развитии, которой гражданско-политической культуры. Коррупция - это процесс и взаимоотношение и, следовательно, государство, государственное управление и граждане разделяют всю ответственность в предотвращении и контролировании коррупции, хотя не в таких пределах.

Граждане и полиция: формирование доверия в процессе демократизации

Самый низкий уровень удовлетворения граждан деятельностью полиции представлен в странах, находящихся в переходной стадии и в Латинской Америке. Действительно, в действиях МИЖП за исключением Словении в 1992, не было ни одной страны в переходной стадии, в которой большинство граждан были бы довольны полицией, в среднем, около 23% удовлетвореных и около 40% недовольных граждан. Кроме того, заявления в полицию о случаях краж и нападений является самым низким из всех случаях, хотя это не те случаи для грабителей; склонность подачи заявлений в полицию, не увеличилась в большинстве стран, находящихся в стадии перехода. Итак, один из наиболее сильных показателей изменения срока формирования доверия между гражданскими лицами и полицией в странах в переходной стадии не обеспечивает удовлетворительную картину.

Оценка деятельности полиции кажется разумным процессом в соотвествующем контексте. Жертвы, ожидающие интересные и эффективные действия от полиции в развитых странах, выражают заботу о гражданских правах, хорошей сервисе и доставке полицией и уверенность в механизме безопасности при возмещении ущерба. Возврат украденной собственности и передача преступника правосудию является разумным откликом жертвы в менее богатом, менее безопасном и более криминально-преступном обществе. Нет сомнения в том, что удовлетворение о деятельности полиции выше в развитом мире и в более зажиточных регионах. Здесь, другие государственные службы, может быть более доступны и высшего качества.

Согласно предотвращению и контролю преступления, МИЖП подтверждает, что общественная безопасность, это всё равно остаётся деятельностью полиции и граждане в странах в переходной стадии ожидают большего присутствия полиции и более эффективных действий от полиции, как минимум. Стремление к безопасности, к меньшей преступности и малому страху преступлений - это процесс, в котором все стороны должны принять участие.

Такое появление есть строгое взаимоотношение между деятельностей полиции, заявлением о преступлениях и частотой патрулирований. Такие обнаружения строго поддерживают идею, как элементарного требования хорошей деятельности в предотвращении престулений, систематическое присутствие полиции, которое увеличивает, как чувство безопасности среди граждан, так и удовлетворение полицией. Излишне говорить, что оба они, каждый по-своему, важен для общественной безопасности.Увеличивается чувство безопасности благодаря присутствию полиции, растёт удовлетворение и доверие масс к полиции. Дело не в больших инвестициях в число персонала и/или оборудования, или не только это. Также, дело в более разумной политике для распределения ресурсов, и ещё больше, дело в основной демократизации общественного института и служб, где надо быть более чувствительными к нуждам клиентов и быть подотчётным общественности. Дело также в изменении культуры взаимоотношений между полицией и гражданами. Подобное изменение требует в тоже время, как более или менее то, что обусловленная профессиональная подготовка, лучшее оборудование и различные виды помощи должны быть предоставлены. Возникает недовольство полицией особенно при подаче заявлений и контроля жилых районов. Страх о том, что могут ограбить в ближайшем будущем, широко распространён. Несмотря на вклады в реформу полиции, общие результаты, согласно оценке граждан и жертв, далеко от удовлетворения. Граждане задумываются о результатах, о каждодневном поведении полиции и культуре полиции в целом. Всё это играет роль в широком контексте социально-экономических и политических изменений и развитии службы ориентации и практики государственного управления, включая полицию.

Полиция должна сосредотачиваться на улучшении результатов в организации: снижении процента издевательств, улучшении понимания безопасности и уровня проблем безопасности, подчерпнутый от населения, предупреждение общественных проблем и улучшение доверия к полиции. Достижение данных целей, это рациональная мера деятельности полиции и её оценке. Граждане оценивая полицию разумно размышляют о преступлениях и поведения полиции на службе обществу. Для предотвращения и контроля преступлений и для правосудия в обществе, оценка граждан по крайней мере так важно как другой-нибудь инструмент для внутренних измерений успехов полиции. Много пожеланий для изменений в культуре полиции и улучшении отношений между полицией и обществом в странах в переходной стадии.

МИЖП - это важный инструмент исследования для отбора и оценки настоящего и для идентификации направления будущей работы. С этих пор, данный запрос для стран, находящихся в переходной стадии, развить их собственные исследования и способствовать публичному обсуждению касающихся преступлений, и также присоединение к следующим действиям МИЖП.

Selected Key Publications on the
International Crime Victim Survey

Alvazzi del Frate Anna, *Manual for the Conduct of the Face-to-face ICVS*. UNICRI, 1996.

Alvazzi del Frate Anna, "Preventing Crime: Citizens' Experiences across the World". UNICRI *Issues & Reports* No. 9, 1997.

Alvazzi del Frate Anna, *Victims of Crime in the Developing World*. UNICRI, 1998.

Alvazzi del Frate Anna, Ugljesa Zvekic, Jan J.M. van Dijk (Eds.), *Understanding Crime: Experiences of Crime and Crime Control*. UNICRI Publ. No. 49, 1993.

Alvazzi del Frate Anna, Angela Patrignani, "Women's Victimisation in the Developing World". UNICRI *Issues & Reports* No. 5, 1995.

Aromaa Kauko, Andri Ahven, *Victims of Crime in Two Baltic Countries: Finnish and Estonian Data from the 1992/1993 International Crime Victimization Survey*. Helsinki: National Research Institute of Legal Policy, 1993.

Aromaa Kauko, Markku Heiskanen, *The Victims of Crime 1992: Preliminary Finnish Data from the 1992 International Crime Victimization Survey*. Helsinki: National Research Institute of Legal Policy, 1992.

Bruinsma Gerben J.N., H.G. van de Bunt, J.P.S. Fiselier, "Quelques Réflexions Théoriques et Méthodologiques à Propos d'une

Recherche Internationale Comparée de Victimation". *Déviance et Société*, 16:1, 1992, pp. 46-68.

Hatalak Oksanna, Anna Alvazzi del Frate, Ugljesa Zvekic (Eds.). *The International Crime Victim Survey in Countries in Transition: National Reports*. UNICRI Publ. No. 62, 1998.

Marenin Otwin, "Victimization Surveys and the Accuracy and Reliability of Official Crime Data in Developing Countries". *Journal of Criminal Justice*, 25:6, 1997, pp. 463-475.

Mayhew Pat, "Findings from the International Crime Survey". *Research Findings No. 8*. London: Home Office Research and Statistics Directorate, 1994.

Mayhew Pat, Jan J.M. van Dijk, *Criminal Victimisation in Eleven Industrialised Countries*. The Hague: Ministry of Justice of the Netherlands, Department of Crime Prevention, WODC, 1997.

van Dijk Jan J.M., "Understanding Crime Rates", *British Journal of Criminology* 34:2, 1994.

van Dijk Jan J.M., "Opportunities of Crime: A Test of the Rational-Interactionist Model". *Crime and Economy - Reports Presented to the 11th Criminological Colloquium (1994)*, Council of Europe, Criminological Research, Vol. XXXII, 1995.

van Dijk Jan J.M., Pat Mayhew, *Criminal Victimization in the Industrialized World: Key Findings of the 1989 and 1992 International Crime Surveys*. The Hague: Ministry of Justice of the Netherlands, Department of Crime Prevention, WODC, 1992.

van Dijk Jan J.M., Pat Mayhew, Martin Killias, *Experiences of Crime Across the World.* Deventer: Kluwer, 1990.

van Dijk Jan J.M., John N. van Kesteren, "The Prevalence and Perceived Seriousness of Victimisation by Crime; Some Results of the International Crime Victim Survey". *European Journal of Crime, Criminal Law and Criminal Justice*, January: 48-71, 1996.

Zvekic Ugljesa, "Policing and Attitudes towards Police in Countries in Transition". In, Pagon Milan (Ed.), *Policing in Central and Eastern Europe, Proceedings of the International Conference.* Ljubljana, Slovenia, 14-16 November 1996.

Zvekic Ugljesa, "International Crime (Victim) Survey: Comparative Advantages and Disadvantages". *International Criminal Justice Review*, Vol. 6, 1996.

Zvekic Ugljesa, "Les Attitudes des Victimes envers la Police et la Punitivité: Résultats des Sondages Internationaux de Victimisation". *Revue Internationale de Criminologie et de Police Technique*, Vol. I, Janvier-Mars, 1997.

Zvekic Ugljesa, *Criminal Victimisation in Countries in Transition.* UNICRI Publ. No. 61, 1998.

Zvekic Ugljesa, Anna Alvazzi del Frate (Eds.), *Criminal Victimisation in the Developing World.* UNICRI Publ. No. 55, 1995.

Zvekic Ugljesa, Boyan Stankov (Eds.), "Victims of Crime in the Balkan Countries". UNICRI *Issues & Reports* No. 11, 1998.

List of UNICRI publications
and staff papers

Publ. No. 1	Tendencias y necesidades de la investigación criminológica en America Latina. (1969) 60p. F. Ferracuti and R. Bergalli. (*)
Publ. No. 2	Manpower and training in the field of social defence. (1970) 152p. F. Ferracuti and M.C. Giannini. (1) (*)
S.P. No. 1	Co-ordination of interdisciplinary research in criminology. (1971) 44p. F. Ferracuti. (*)
Publ. No. 3	Social defence in Uganda: A survey of research. (1971) 129p. (*)
Publ. No. 4	Public et justice: Une étude pilote en Tunisie. (1971) 186p. A. Bouhdiba. (*)
S.P. No. 2.	The evaluation and improvement of manpower training programmes in social defence. (1972) 33p. R.W. Burnham. (1) (*)
S.P. No. 3.	Perceptions of deviance: Suggestions for cross-cultural research. (1972) 84p. G. Newman. (*)
S.P. No. 4.	Perception clinique et psychologique de la déviance. F. Ferracuti and G. Newman. Sexual deviance: A sociological analysis. G. Newman. Aspetti sociali dei comportamenti devianti sessuali. (1973) 75p. F. Ferracuti and R. Lazzari. (*)
S.P. No. 5.	Psychoactive drug control: Issues and recommendations. (1973) 98p. J.J. Moore, C.R.B. Joyce and J. Woodcock. (1) (*)
Publ. No. 5	Migration: Report of the research conference on migration, ethnic minority status and social adaptation, Rome, 13-16 June 1972. 196p. (*)
Publ. No. 6	A programme for drug use research: Report of the proceedings of a Workshop at Frascati, Italy, 11-15 December 1972. 40p. (*)
S.P. No. 6	Un programma di ricerca sulla droga. Rapporto del seminario di Frascati, Italy, 11-15 dicembre 1972. 93p. (*)
Publ. No. 7	A world directory of criminological institutes. (1974) 152p. B. Kasme (ed.). (*)
Publ. No. 8	Recent contributions to Soviet criminology. (1974) 126p. (*)

Publ. No. 9   Economic crisis and crime: Interim report and materials. (1974) 115p. (*)

Publ. No. 10   Criminological research and decision-making: Studies on the influence of criminological research on criminal policy in The Netherlands and Finland. (1974) 220p. (*)

Publ. No. 11   Evaluation research in criminal justice: Material and proceedings of a research conference convened in the context of the Fifth United Nations Congress for the Prevention of Crime and the Treatment of Offenders. (1976) 321p. (*)

Publ. No. 12   Juvenile justice: An international survey, country reports, related materials and suggestions for future research. (1976) 251p. (*)

Publ. No. 13   The protection of the artistic and archaeological heritage: A view from Italy and India. (1976) 259p. (*)

Publ. No. 14   Prison architecture: An international survey of representative closed institutions and analysis of current trends in prison design. (1974) 238p. (2) (*)

Publ. No. 15   Economic crises and crime: Correlations between the state of the economy, deviance and the control of deviance. (1976) 243p. (*)

Publ. No. 16   Investigating drug abuse: A multinational programme of pilot studies into a non-medical use of drugs. (1976) 192p. J.J. Moore. (*)

Publ No. 17   A world directory of criminological institutes. (2nd edition) (1978) 521p. (*)

Publ. No. 18   Delay in the administration of criminal justice: India. (1978) 73p. S.K. Mukherjee and A. Gupta. (*)

Publ. No. 19   Research on drug policy. (1979) 93p. J.J. Moore and L. Bozzetti. (*)

The effect of Islamic legislation on crime prevention in Saudi Arabia. (1981) 606p. (3) (*)

Publ. No. 20   A world directory of criminological institutes. (3rd edition) (1982) 691p. (*)

Publ. No. 21   Combatting drug abuse. (1984) 251p. F. Bruno. (*)

Publ. No. 22   Juvenile social maladjustment and human rights in the context of development. (1984) 504p. (*)

Publ. No. 23   The phenomenology of kidnappings in Sardinia. (1984) 211p. I.F. Caramazza and U. Leone. (*)

126

Publ. No. 24   The role of the judge in contemporary society. (1984) 80p. (4) (*)

Publ. No. 25   Crime and criminal policy: Papers in honour of Manuel López-Rey. (1985) 747p. P. David (ed.). (*)

Publ. No. 26   First Joint International Conference on Research in Crime Prevention. Riyadh, 23-25 January 1984 235p. (5) (*)

Publ. No. 27   Action-oriented research on youth crime: An international perspective. (1986) 275p. U. Zvekic (ed.). (*)

Publ. No. 28   A world directory of criminological institutes. (4th edition). (1986) 582p. C. Masotti Santoro (ed.). (*)

Publ. No. 29   Research and international co-operation in criminal justice: Survey on needs and priorities of developing countries. (1987) 264p. U. Zvekic and A. Mattei. (6)

Publ. No. 30   Drugs and punishment. (1988) 146p. D. Cotic. (6)

Publ. No. 31   Analysing (in)formal mechanisms of crime control: A cross-cultural perspective. (1988) 343p. M. Findlay and U. Zvekic. (6)

Prison in Africa: Acts of the Seminar for Heads of Penitentiary Administrations of African Countries. (1988) 286p. (7) (*)

Publ. No. 32   The death penalty: A bibliographical research. (1988) 320p. (6)

Publ. No. 33   La criminología en America Latina. (1990) 288p. L. Aniyar de Castro (ed.). (6)

Publ. No. 35   A world directory of criminological institutes. (5th edition) (1990) 661p. C. Masotti Santoro (ed.). (6)

Publ. No. 36   Essays on crime and development. (1990) 377p. U. Zvekic (ed.). (6)

Publ. No. 38   Soviet criminology update. (1990) 179p. V.N. Kudriavtzav (ed.). (6)

Publ. No. 39   Diritti umani ed istruzione penale. Corso di formazione sulle tecniche di istruzione ed investigazione. Castelgandolfo, Italy, 11-22 September 1989. 245p. (*)

Publ. No. 40   Infancia y control penal en America Latina. (1990) 417p. E. Garcia Méndez and E. Carranza (eds.). (9)

Publ. No. 41   Toward scientifically based prevention. (1990) 181p. F. Bruno, M.E. Andreotti and M. Brunetti (eds.). (6)

Publ. No. 42   Ser niño en America Latina. De las necesidades a los derechos. (1991) 434p. E. Garcia Mendez and M. del Carmen Bianchi (eds.). (10)

Publ. No. 43   Compendio per la prevenzione. Vols. I/II/III. (1991) F. Bruno (ed.). (*)

Publ. No. 44   Cocaine today: Its effects on the individual and society. (1991) 420p. F. Bruno (ed.). (11) (*)

Publ. No. 45   Justicia y desarrollo democratico en Italia y America Latina. (1992) 343p. G. Longo, U. Leone and M. Bonomo (eds.). (6)

Publ. No. 46   Development and crime. An exploratory study in Yugoslavia. (1992) 350p. U. Leone, D. Radovanovic and U. Zvekic. (12) (*)

Publ. No. 47   Criminology in Africa. (1992) 272p. T. Mushanga (ed.). (6)

Publ. No. 48   Pathways to the management of mentally-ill offenders in the criminal justice system. (1993) 264p. A. Manna, R. Kurosawa and K. Hamai (eds.). (6)

Publ. No. 49   Understanding crime: Experiences of crime and crime control. (1993) 718p. A. Alvazzi del Frate, U. Zvekic and J.J.M. van Dijk (eds.). (6) (13)

Alternative policing styles: Cross-cultural perspectives (1993) 288p. M. Findlay and U. Zvekic. (14)

Publ. No. 50   Environmental crime, sanctioning strategies and sustainable development. (1993) 422p. A. Alvazzi del Frate and J. Norberry (eds.). (6) (15)

Human rights and crime prevention. (1993) 144p. U. Leone and A. Patrignani (eds.). (16)

Publ. No. 51   Criminologia internazionale. (1993) 670p. U. Leone. (6)

Alternatives to imprisonment in comparative perspective. (1994) 464p. U. Zvekic (ed.). (17)

Alternatives to imprisonment in comparative perspective: Bibliography. (1994) 537p. U. Zvekic and A. Alvazzi del Frate (eds.). (17)

Publ. No. 52   Crime and crime prevention in Moscow. (1994) 176p. M. Alexeyeva and A. Patrignani (eds.). (6) (18)

Publ. No. 53   Development and policy use of criminal justice information. (1995) 530p. U. Zvekic, L. Wang and R. Scherpenzeel (eds.). (6)

Publ. No. 54   A world directory of criminological institutes. (6th edition) (1995) 661p. C. Masotti Santoro (ed.). (6)

Changements sociaux, criminalité et victimisation en Tunisie. (1995) 412p. R. Villé (comp.). (19)

Publ. No. 55	Criminal victimisation in the developing world. (1995) 434p. U. Zvekic and A. Alvazzi del Frate (eds.). (6)

Probation round the world: A comparative study. (1995) 233p. K. Hamai, R. Villé, R. Harris, M. Hough and U. Zvekic (eds.). (20)

Publ. No. 56	Environmental protection at national and international levels: potentials and limits of criminal justice. (1997) G. Heine, M. Prabhu and A. Alvazzi del Frate (eds.). (21)
Publ. No. 57	Victims of crime in the developing world. (1998) 150p. A. Alvazzi del Frate. (6)
Publ. No. 58	Promoting probation internationally. (1998) 250 p. R. Villé, U. Zvekic and J.F. Klaus (eds.).
Publ. No. 59	Rromani youths: The pathways of juvenile justice. (1998) 180 p. A. Patrignani and R. Villé (eds.).
Publ. No. 60	Handbook on probation services: Guidelines for probation practitioners and managers. (1998) 190 p. J.F. Klaus.
Publ. No. 61	Criminal victimisation in countries in transition. (1998) 144 p. U. Zvekic.
Publ. No. 62	International Crime Victim Survey in countries in transition: National reports. (1998) O. Hatalak, A. Alvazzi del Frate and U. Zvekic (eds.).

Issues & Reports / *Thèmes & Rapports*

No. 1/1994	Latent crime in Russia *La criminalité latente en Russie (*)*
No. 2/1994	Police training in drug abuse prevention *La formation de la police pour la prévention de l'abus des drogues*
No. 3/1994	Papua New Guinea: crime and criminal justice information *Papouasie-Nouvelle-Guinée: informations sur la criminalité et la justice pénale*
No. 4/1995	Violence in the family *La violence dans la famille (*)*
No. 5/1995	Women's victimisation in developing countries *La victimisation des femmes dans les pays en développement*

No. 6/1996	Child abuse. Some reflections based on the situation in six European countries
	L'Enfance maltraitée. Quelques réflexions basées sur la situation dans six pays européens
No. 7-8/1997	Crime in Southern Africa: Towards the Year 2000
	La Criminalité en Afrique australe: vers l'an 2000
No. 9/1997	Preventing crime: Citizens' experience across the world
	Prévenir la criminalité: L'expérience des citoyens à travers le monde
No. 10/1997	Combating Corruption in Central and Eastern Europe
	La lutte contre la corruption en Europe Centrale et de l'Est
No. 11/1998	Victims of Crime in the Balkan Region
	Les victimes de la criminalité dans la région des Balkans

Notes

(*)   Out of print.

(1)   Also published in French and Spanish.

(2)   Available through The Architectural Press, 9 Queen Anne's Gate, London SWH 9BY, England.

(3)   At the request of the Government of The Kingdom of Saudi Arabia, UNSDRI published English, French and Spanish editions of this publication.

(4)   In collaboration with the International Association of Judges.

(5)   In collaboration with the Arab Security Studies and Training Center in Riyadh, The Kingdom of Saudi Arabia.

(6)   Available through United Nations Publications in Geneva (Palais des Nations, CH-1211 Geneva 10, Switzerland) or New York (United Nations Headquarters, Room A3315, New York, N.Y. 10017, U.S.A.).

(7)   In collaboration with the Ministry of Justice of Italy and the International Centre for Sociological, Penal and Penitentiary Studies, Messina, Italy.

(9)   Joint UNICRI/ILANUD publication.

(10) In collaboration with the UNICEF, ILANUD, IIN (Instituto Interamericano del Niño) and DNI (Defensa de los Niños International).

(11) Also published in Italian.

(12) Joint UNICRI/IKSI publication.

(13) Joint UNICRI/Dutch Ministry of Justice/Italian Ministry of the Interior publication.

(14) Available through Kluwer, Law and Taxation Publisher, P.O. Box 23 7400 GA Deventer, The Netherlands.

(15)   In collaboration with the Australian Institute of Criminology.

(16)   Joint UNICRI/Ministry of Justice (Malta) publication.

(17)   Available through Nelson-Hall Publishers, Chicago, Illinois, USA.

(18)   Joint UNICRI/Research Institute of the Russian Ministry of the Interior publication.

(19)   Joint UNICRI/INTES publication. Available through CERP, Tunis, Tunisia.

(20)   Available through Routledge, London, UK.

(21)   In collaboration with The Max-Planck-Institut für ausländisches und internationales Strafrecht, Freiburg; published by: Edition Iuscrim, Freiburg I. B., Germany.

United Nations
Interregional Crime and
Justice Research Institute

via Giulia 52, 00186 Rome, Italy
Tel: (+39 6) 6877437   **Fax:** (+39 6) 6892638
E-mail: unicri@unicri.it
www: http://www.unicri.it